Determining the Status and Trends of Key Invasive Plant Species in the Delaware Water Gap National Recreation Area

Technical Report NPS/NER/NRTR—2009/134

Bradley A. Eichelberger and Stephanie J. Perles

Pennsylvania Natural Heritage Program
Western Pennsylvania Conservancy
208 Airport Drive
Middletown, PA 17057

February 2009

U.S. Department of the Interior
National Park Service
Northeast Region
Philadelphia, Pennsylvania

The Northeast Region of the National Park Service (NPS) comprises national parks and related areas in 13 New England and Mid-Atlantic states. The diversity of parks and their resources are reflected in their designations as national parks, seashores, historic sites, recreation areas, military parks, memorials, and rivers and trails. Biological, physical, and social science research results, natural resource inventory and monitoring data, scientific literature reviews, bibliographies, and proceedings of technical workshops and conferences related to these park units are disseminated through the NPS/NER Technical Report (NRTR) and Natural Resources Report (NRR) series. The reports are a continuation of series with previous acronyms of NPS/PHSO, NPS/MAR, NPS/BSO-RNR, and NPS/NERBOST. Individual parks may also disseminate information through their own report series.

Natural Resources Reports are the designated medium for information on technologies and resource management methods; "how to" resource management papers; proceedings of resource management workshops or conferences; and natural resource program descriptions and resource action plans.

Technical Reports are the designated medium for initially disseminating data and results of biological, physical, and social science research that addresses natural resource management issues; natural resource inventories and monitoring activities; scientific literature reviews; bibliographies; and peer-reviewed proceedings of technical workshops, conferences, or symposia.

Mention of trade names or commercial products does not constitute endorsement or recommendation for use by the National Park Service.

This report was accomplished under Cooperative Agreement 4506060766, Task Agreement 005, with assistance from the NPS. The statements, findings, conclusions, recommendations, and data in this report are solely those of the author(s), and do not necessarily reflect the views of the U.S. Department of the Interior, National Park Service.

Print copies of reports in these series, produced in limited quantity and only available as long as the supply lasts, or preferably, file copies on CD, may be obtained by sending a request to the address on the back cover. Print copies also may be requested from the NPS Technical Information Center (TIC), Denver Service Center, PO Box 25287, Denver, CO 80225-0287. A copy charge may be involved. To order from TIC, refer to document D-303.

This report may also be available as a downloadable portable document format file from the Internet at http://www.nps.gov/nero/science/.

Please cite this publication as:

Eichelberger, B. A., and S. J. Perles. February 2009. Determining the Status and Trends of Key Invasive Plant Species in the Delaware Water Gap National Recreation Area. Technical Report NPS/NER/NRTR—2009/134. National Park Service. Philadelphia, PA.

Table of Contents

Figures

Figures (continued)

Tables

Appendixes

Acknowledgments

We would like to thank the following people for their time and assistance with this project at the Delaware Water Gap National Recreational Area. Jeff Shreiner, Kathy Commisso, and Leslie Morlock provided valuable information concerning previous research projects and locations of invasive species occurrences. Matt Marshall, Jennifer Keefer, Jeffery Shreiner, Greg Podniesinski, and John Young provided valuable time in reviewing and critiquing this document. Appreciation goes to the Pennsylvania and New York Natural Heritage programs for their assistance in collection of data used for analyses, particularly Greg Podniesinski, Amanda Treher, Greg Edinger, and Aissa Feldmann. The project was funded by the National Park Service's Eastern Rivers and Mountain Network.

Executive Summary

Invasive exotic plants pose a serious threat to the natural resources of many national parks. Invasive species can displace native plant species, inhibit the regeneration of native forest trees, degrade habitats for rare species, and alter vegetation community structure and composition. Due to these potentially serious impacts; the status, trends, and early detection of invasive species is currently considered a Tier 1 vital sign for terrestrial ecosystems in the Eastern Rivers and Mountains Inventory and Monitoring Network.

Data regarding invasive species were collected for the Delaware Water Gap National Recreation Area (DEWA) and Upper Delaware Scenic and Recreational River (UPDE) during vegetation mapping efforts from 2003 through 2006. National Park Service natural resource managers and biologists provided a list of 61 target invasive species to be included in the surveys. Prior to the surveys, National Park Service natural resource managers and biologists classified the status of the target species as either present (confirmed locations), encroaching (believed to be non-existent), or unconfirmed within DEWA. During the vegetation mapping field work, the presence and abundance of the 61 targeted invasive species were recorded at each vegetation classification plot and accuracy assessment point. If a species did not occur at a sampling point, its absence at that point was recorded. Percent cover for the target species was collected within a 50-m (164-ft) radius of the sampling point. Data were collected at 1,355 sampling points throughout DEWA, including 251 vegetation classification plots and 1,104 accuracy assessment points. In UPDE, data was collected at 771 sampling points including 232 vegetation classification plots and 539 accuracy assessment points. Data on all 61 invasive exotic species were summarized in terms of abundance, frequency, and the number of communities that species had infested.

A subset of the 61 identified invasive species were selected for modeling purposes based on four factors: 1) the species' current distribution and abundance, 2) the severity of the species' potential ecological impact, 3) the species' life history traits and its ability to spread, and 4) the difficulty in managing or eradicating the species. The observed species abundance and distribution and park-specific management objectives and priorities were considered in the selection of species. Natural resource managers from the park and other regional National Park Service scientists were consulted during the selection process. From this process, 11 species and one vegetation community type were selected for parkwide predictive modeling.

Data was pooled for both DEWA and UPDE to increase sample sizes for species. Only sample points that had an abundance of occasional or abundant percent cover were used for this analysis in order to offset spatial errors. Due to the ability of maximum entropy modeling in handling low sample sizes, maximum entropy models using the Maxent software program were built for tree-of-heaven (*Ailanthus altissima*), Japanese barberry (*Berberis thunbergii*), spotted knapweed (*Centaurea biebersteinii*), winged euonymus (*Euonymus alatus*), Japanese hops (*Humulus japonicus*), common reed (*Phragmites australis*), mile-a-minute (*Polygonum perfoliatum*), and common mullein (*Verbascum thapsus*). Environmental variables related to vegetation community, soil moisture, and light availability were extracted to species occurrence locations using GIS software. A correlation matrix was used to test for co-linearity between environmental variables for each species. If variables were correlated ($p < 0.05$) and had a

Pearson's correlation value greater then 0.700, variables were reduced to avoid multi-collinearity and over-fitting of the model. The remaining environmental variables were included in the maximum entropy models and 25% of the occurrence data was randomly withheld for each species as an evaluation dataset to test model validity. The models were used to build distribution maps for invasive species within the park.

Heuristic models were built for Norway maple (*Acer platanoides*), narrowleaf bittercress (*Cardamine impatiens*), and fig buttercup (*Ranunculus ficaria*) due to excessively small sample sizes. The models were built based upon the species' habitat preferences derived from scientific literature. All data layers were overlaid in GIS and suitable habitat was delineated where all the parameters overlapped. In order to fully evaluate the model's performance for each species, any known presence points and 1,000 randomly sampled points containing absence data from the vegetation mapping efforts were used.

Model accuracy was calculated for both the model (training) and evaluation (testing) datasets based on the overall accuracy (percentage of correctly predicted known presence and absence points), error of commission (percentage of false positives), error of omissions (percentage of false negatives), and the True Skill Statistic (TSS). TSS is an index that compares the observed agreement against what is expected by chance. This measure measures from 1.0 (perfect agreement) to -1.0 (complete disagreement). Maximum entropy uses only presence data and pseudo-absences, randomly sampled background data treated as an absence dataset. Therefore, error of commission for the modeling dataset cannot be calculated. Heuristic models lack a modeling dataset and were only evaluated on the evaluation data.

Eastern hemlock (*Tsuga canadensis*) communities were ranked using a landscape metric designed to predict the susceptibility of the stand to being invaded by exotic plant species. This metric incorporates canopy gaps and area of edge influence as well as the number and abundance of invasive plant species within hemlock stands and their adjacent forest stands. Community scores were developed in order to quantify the amount of degradation within that community polygon. All community polygons within the park boundaries were given a categorical score for percent canopy cover, percent edge, invasive species abundance, and number of invasive species so that each category score ranged from zero to four. If the community did not have a sampling point recorded for invasive species, only the percent canopy cover and percent edge were averaged to formulate the community score.

To further understand current invasive species' distributions, all vegetation communities were ranked based on an infestation index to derive areas of high and low invasive activity. Vegetation community polygons (n=1,204) were given an infestation value based on the abundance per sampling point and species per sampling point rank values derived in the eastern hemlock community analysis. The abundance and species ranks were averaged to give an infestation index. The resulting index is indicative of the community's current invasion status. Rare communities were addressed in this analysis to identify areas where park managers may wish to concentrate invasive species management efforts.

Overall, the accuracy assessment and modeling data suggests invasive exotic plant species are not completely ubiquitous but certainly present within Delaware Water Gap National Recreation Area. Based on the accuracy assessment points, it appears a large portion of the park contained few invasive species. None of the individual models predicted greater than 35% of the park as potentially suitable habitat for each given species. However, collectively, the distribution models predicted 59% of the park as potential habitat. The results suggest the park is in need of extensive invasive species management.

Invasive species tended to exhibit certain patterns within the park. Areas of high invasive activity appear to be associated with successional areas, such as regenerating forests and agricultural fields, as well as riparian and mesic terrestrial forests. These habitats provide light availability and mesic conditions that appear to be preferred by the invasive species. It is important to note that most native species would proliferate from these conditions as well; however, such species are typically outcompeted by invasive species. Areas of low invasive activity appear to be cliff complexes and dry terrestrial communities. Such communities are well-drained to drought-prone and may not satisfy the soil moisture preference that invasive species seem to exhibit. Rare communities that tended to have a higher mean invasive index were habitats with rich, mesic conditions such as fens and riverside rock outcrops but also some scree slopes which offer high light availability. Given the rarity of these communities, efforts should be concentrated on invasive species management at these sites and the surrounding communities.

The maximum entropy models tend to best represent potential distributions within the park, based on model evaluation results. Japanese barberry, winged euonymus, and tree-of-heaven were the most widely predicted of the target species. This is probably due to broader habitat preferences of these species when compared to the other species modeled with maximum entropy. For example, Japanese barberry and winged euonymus can grow in a variety of soil and light conditions while common reed is typically restricted to wet communities. All species in this modeling method appear to have moderate accuracy based on the measures of model performance with a few exceptions. Japanese barberry and winged euonymus had higher rates of test commission and omission which resulted in lower true skill statistics (TSS). This may be a result of these two species having a broad range of habitat tolerances which the model was unable to compensate for or an important variable was overlooked in the modeling process. In general, sample size appears to increase accuracy with these models. For example, the *A. altissima* model had a considerably lower percent test omission error, lower test commission error, and higher TSS compared to *C. biebersteinii* and *E. alatus*.

The heuristic models, in general, represent plausible distributions of invasive species within the park. For species within this modeling approach, the results suggest that the modeled distributions are accurately predicted with the exception of *Acer platanoides*. *A. platanoides* had a considerably high test omission error and low TSS value, most likely due to the small test sample size for occurrences (n=3). However for this modeling approach, the overall accuracy score is more biased towards the absence data used to test the model due to low sample sizes or lack of presence data to test the models. Ideally, these models should be evaluated using more presence data but could be used to guide future surveys for these species.

Although the models appear to be fairly accurate in prediction, several caveats need to be taken into consideration when interpreting the results. Maximum entropy distribution maps are data dependent and are subjected to biases contained in the data (such as sampling data not addressing the full range of habitat preferences for the species). The environmental drivers for the species may be an artifact of the data and may not reflect actual ecological significance. Such a variable may fit the data very well and not be representative of a habitat preference or requirement. It is possible that a vegetation community, which was consistently the most important driver for all maximum entropy models, could be an artifact variable but it is more likely the communities are a combination of environmental and biotic variables such as seral stage, soil moisture, mycorrhizal associations, and the inability of the associated vegetation to outcompete invasive species. While the vegetation layer certainly refines the models in terms of the predicted outcome, it is still possible to predict coarser invasive species' distributions without a vegetation community data layer. The heuristic models are based on expert knowledge and therefore may not fully address the habitat variables that restrict a species' distribution. This would account for the large amount of predicted area for these species, given certain limiting variables are currently not incorporated. Additionally these models are completely data independent in the statistical sense and may be subject to biases made on expert's assumptions.

Several management recommendations can be provided based on this study. We suggest efforts should be concentrated at species modeled using maximum entropy, given known ocurrences are more frequent within the park and considered an immediate threat. Based upon the model and accuracy assessment results, Japanese barberry appears to be the most widespread species throughout the park and may pose considerable threats to natural resources. However, given the breadth of the *B. thunbergii*'s distribution within the park, it may be more beneficial to concentrate efforts where other species overlap with *B. thunbergii*. Additionally, while tree-of-heaven appears to be one of the most widespread of these species and should therefore be considered a priority, it can often be difficult to manage, given the ability to reproduce via clonal growth. More restricted species, such as *Verbascum thapsus*, *Centaurea biebersteinii*, and *Phragmites australis,* had lower predicted distributions, given their habitat preferences, so it may be more beneficial to target areas where these species are concentrated versus a species that occurs in multiple conditions across the park. Species modeled via heuristic models are currently not frequent in the park but appear to have a potentially large distribution. Therefore, it may be beneficial to establish monitoring plots and/or survey routes in areas where these species were predicted to occur. Rare communities and areas of high resource value should also be given priority. However, it is important to utilize appropriate measures of control to limit the disturbances of the native communities where invasive species occur. Overall, several of these species may be managed at one time by targeting areas of high infestation, such as successional, riparian, and mesic terrestrial forests. Areas with a large number of overlapping distributions include areas near Milford, Minisink Island, Namanock Island, Dingman's Ferry, south of Shapnack Island, Bushkill Creek, Depew Island, Poxono Island, Depue Island, Brodhead Creek, and the New Jersey portion of the park adjacent to Arrow Island.

The model for susceptibility of eastern hemlock communities to invasion suggests that *T. canadensis* communities in DEWA are currently at a moderate risk to invasion. Overall, the *T. canadensis* communities are currently minimally invaded with a few sites degraded by invasive species. The spatial distribution of these communities shows that the majority of them are situated in fairly intact forest complexes. It appears that *T. canadensis* communities adjacent to successional, riparian, and mesic terrestrial communities had a higher index value, indicating a higher susceptibility to invasion. Such results are most likely related to higher light availability and mesic conditions. However, these results are static and do not predict future changes in canopy cover that would provide the light availability required for invasive plant species.

According to the eastern hemlock analysis, several areas of hemlock stands may be targeted for monitoring and management of invasive species following hemlock woolly adelgid infestations. Areas in most danger include stand complexes located at the mouth of Conashaugh Creek, mouth of Dingmans Creek, Little and Big Bushkill creeks, as well as many isolated or smaller stands, especially along the Delaware River or adjacent to developed areas such as Milford, 209/206 interchange, Cliff Park Inn, Delaware Water Gap boro, and the water gap itself. Moderate to highly susceptible areas include the Raymondskill drainage, most of Dingmans Creek, Broadhead-Heller Creek, Mill Creek, and Toms Creek. In addition, the Eastern Hemlock Forests have inherently greater susceptibility to invasive plants than the mixed hemlock types if widespread hemlock decline or mortality continues. Of the 53 Eastern Hemlock Forest polygons, 19 polygons have a Susceptibility Index > 1.5 (greater than average), so these areas might be targeted for monitoring or management.

Introduction

Invasive exotic plants pose a serious threat to the natural resources of many national parks. Invasive species can displace native plant species, inhibit the regeneration of native forest trees, degrade habitats for rare species, and alter vegetation community structure and composition (Vitousek et al. 1996). Due to these potentially serious impacts; the status, trends, and early detection of invasive species is currently considered a Tier 1 vital sign for terrestrial ecosystems in the Eastern Rivers and Mountains Inventory and Monitoring Network (Marshall and Piekielek 2007).

In order to effectively protect the parks' natural resources, invasive plant species must be managed. However, management of these species typically requires more time and financial resources than is available to the parks. Prioritization of resources for invasive species management is therefore essential to protect a park's natural resources.

The first step in effectively managing a park's invasive plant species is an assessment of the status of the invasive plants within the park. In parks that cover tens of thousands of hectares, such as Delaware Water Gap National Recreation Area, assessing the presence, abundance, and distribution of invasive plants is an enormous task. One efficient way to estimate the distribution of invasive species in these large parks is through predictive modeling. Predictive models correlate species presence and absence data with environmental variables to produce the probability of a species occurring under a set of environmental conditions. A threshold probability is usually chosen based on several assessment methods then applied to the model so that any probability above the threshold is considered a predicted occurrence or suitable habitat (Guisan and Zimmerman 2000).

Several methods for predicting species distributions exist in the scientific literature and include, but are not limited to, logistic regression (Pereira and Itami 1991; Mladenoff et al. 1995; Orrock et al. 1999; Zimmerman and Kienast 1999; Collingham et al. 2000; Carmel et al. 2001; Chamblin et al. 2004), classification and regression trees (CART) (Lees and Ritman 1991; Moore et al. 1991; Franklin 1998; Iverson and Prasad 1998; Taverna et al. 2004), maximum entropy (Elith et al. 2006; Hernandez et al. 2006; Pearson et al. 2007; Phillips et al. 2006), and heuristic models (Wu and Smeins 2000). Each modeling method has associated weaknesses and strengths. A common problem with modeling species has been low sample sizes, which tend to skew data distributions in modeling methods such as classification and regression trees (CART) and logistic regression (Hernandez et al. 2006). Maximum entropy, a modeling method that uses maximum likelihood measures, has been used to successfully model species with low sample sizes (Elith et al. 2006; Hernandez et al. 2006; Pearson et al. 2007; Phillips et al. 2006). Heuristic modeling, modeling based on expert knowledge of a species, is also useful when accurate field data does not exist; however, this method may be more subject to biases (Wu and Smeins 2000).

Several factors may influence the distribution of invasive exotic species. Species' preferences for soil properties, such as drainage and pH, are important environmental drivers for their occurrence on the landscape (Riefner and Windler 1979; Searcy et al. 2006). Light availability plays an important role in invasive species colonization and forest edges, canopy gaps (Brothers

1

and Spingarn 1992; Matlack 1994; Goldblum and Beatty 1999; Parendes and Jones 2000) and successional stages (Matlack 1993, 1994) provide high light penetration needed for invasive species survival. Stream and road edges act as corridors for dispersal of invasive species and provide suitable habitat for plants and propagules (Parendes and Jones 2000). Additionally, aspect may play an important role in forest edge microclimate in terms of solar radiation and soil moisture (Brothers and Spingarn 1992; Matlack 1994). For example, invasive species were more dominant on north-facing, cooler edges than south-facing, warmer edges in Indiana (Brothers and Spingarn 1992). Modeling invasive exotic species occurrences using environmental variables known to influence distributions will provide insight into the species' potential extent and threats to natural resources.

This project synthesizes a large set of invasive plant abundance and distribution data and uses such data to predict the potential distribution of several high-priority invasive species throughout Delaware Water Gap National Recreation Area. This information can then be used to allocate resources earmarked for invasive species management.

Objectives

Objectives of this project were to assess the status of established and encroaching invasive plant species in the park, model potential trends in parkwide distribution of selected high-priority invasive plant species, and provide recommendations for setting management priorities. Emphasis was placed on modeling selected invasive species, the susceptibility of hemlock communities to potential invasions by exotic plant species, and the overall infestation condition of vegetation communities within the park. Areas of high predictive invasions and rare communities were addressed to identify areas where park managers may wish to concentrate invasive species management efforts.

Methodology

Data Collection and Species Selection for Predictive Distribution Modeling

Data regarding invasive species were collected for the Delaware Water Gap National Recreation Area (DEWA) and Upper Delaware Scenic and Recreational River (UPDE) during vegetation mapping efforts from 2003 through 2006 (Perles et al. 2007; Perles et al. 2008). National Park Service natural resource managers and biologists provided a list of 61 target invasive species to be included in the surveys. Prior to the surveys, National Park Service natural resource managers and biologists classified the status of the target species as either present (confirmed locations), encroaching (no known locations), or unconfirmed within DEWA (Table 1). During the vegetation mapping field work, the presence and abundance of the 61 targeted invasive species were recorded at each vegetation classification plot and accuracy assessment point. If a species did not occur at a sampling point, its absence at that point was recorded. Percent cover for the target species was collected within a 50-m (164-ft) radius of the sampling point. Percent cover was classified as either absent (0% cover in 50-m radius area), rare (one plant or very few widely scattered plants in 50-m radius area), occasional (scattered, approximately 1–20% cover in 50-m radius area), or abundant (very common, approximately >20% cover in 50-m radius area) for each species. Abundance values were assigned for each species using the mean value of the cover class. For example, a species with an abundance of occasional (approximately 1–20% cover) was given a cover percentage/abundance value of 10%. Data were collected at 1,355 sampling points throughout DEWA, including 251 vegetation classification plots and 1,104 accuracy assessment points. In UPDE, data was collected at 771 sampling points including 232 vegetation classification plots and 539 accuracy assessment points. Data on all 61 invasive exotic species were summarized in terms of abundance, frequency, and the number of communities that species had infested.

A subset of the 61 identified invasive species was selected for modeling purposes based on four factors: 1) the species' current distribution and abundance; 2) the severity of species' potential ecological impact; 3) the species' life history traits and its ability to spread; and 4) the difficulty in managing or eradicating the species. NatureServe's Invasive Species Assessment Protocol and I-Ranks (Morse et al. 2004) and the National Park Service's Alien Plant Ranking System (Hiebert and Stubbendieck 1993; Hiebert 1997) were used as guides in this effort. The observed species abundance and distribution and park-specific management objectives and priorities were considered in the selection of species. Natural resource managers from the park and other regional National Park Service scientists were consulted during the selection process.

Based on the number of observed occurrences, species were placed into three modeling scenarios within DEWA (Table 1). Scenario A represents species that are widely distributed throughout the park (occurred at greater than 10% of accuracy assessment points). Species in scenario A may produce accurate distribution models due to robust occurrence data; however, these results may seem intuitive, given the species are already widely distributed.

Scenario B represents species not yet established widely but for which there are known locations in our data set or from National Park Service data (current locations or previous occurrences that were removed). The models would create potential distribution maps that would provide

Table 1. Modeling scenarios, known status, number of sampling points, and percent of total sampling points at which species was present for target invasive species in Delaware Water Gap National Recreation Area.

Modeling Scenario	Scientific Name	Status	Number of Sampling Points at which Species was Present	Percentage of Sampling Points at which Species was Present
Scenario A	*Berberis thunbergii*	Present	467	>10%
	Rosa multiflora	Present	432	
	Microstegium vimineum	Present	369	
	Alliaria petiolata	Present	357	
	Lonicera morrowii	Present	193	
	Elaeagnus umbellata	Present	184	
	Celastrus orbiculatus	Present	95	5–10%
	Lythrum salicaria	Present	91	
	Polygonum cuspidatum	Present	73	
	Ailanthus altissima	Present	62	
	Rubus phoenicolasius	Present	39	1–5%
	Centaurea biebersteinii	Present	34	
	Lonicera japonica	Present	31	
	Euonymus alatus	Present	31	
	Verbascum thapsus	Present	31	
	Ligustrum spp.	Present	21	
	Phragmites australis	Present	18	
	Hesperis matronalis	Present	18	
Scenario B	*Elaeagnus angustifolia*	Present	12	<1%
	Vinca minor	Present	11	
	Coronilla varia	Present	9	
	Lonicera tatarica	Present	9	
	Lonicera maackii	Present	8	
	Wisteria sinensis	Present	6	
	Rhamnus cathartica	Present	5	
	Eupatorium serotinum	Present	4	
	Acer platanoides	Present	3	
	Carduus nutans	Present	3	
	Cirsium arvense	Present	3	
	Tussilago farfara	Present	2	
	Paulownia tomentosa	Present	2	
	Polygonum perfoliatum	Present	2	
	Myriophyllum spicatum	Present	1	
	Akebia quinata	Present	1	
	Polygonum sachalinense	Present	1	
	Lychnis flos-cuculi	Present	1	

Table 1. Modeling scenarios, known status, number of sampling points, and percent of total sampling points at which species was present for target invasive species in Delaware Water Gap National Recreation Area (continued).

Modeling Scenario	Scientific Name	Status	Number of Sampling Points at which Species was Present	Percentage of Sampling Points at which Species was Present
Scenario C	Acer palmatum	Present	0	Absent
	Albizia julibrissin	Present	0	
	Anthriscus sylvestris	Present	0	
	Cabomba caroliniana	Present	0	
	Hedera helix	Present	0	
	Lespedeza cuneata	Present	0	
	Potamogeton crispus	Present	0	
	Wisteria floribunda	Present	0	
	Myriophyllum heterophyllum	Unconfirmed	0	
	Ampelopsis brevipedunculata	Encroach	0	
	Cardamine impatiens	Encroach	0	
	Cynanchum louiseae	Encroach	0	
	Cynanchum rossicum	Encroach	0	
	Egeria densa	Encroach	0	
	Frangula alnus	Encroach	0	
	Heracleum mantegazzianum	Encroach	0	
	Humulus japonicus	Encroach	0	
	Hydrilla verticillata	Encroach	0	
	Phellodendron japonicum	Encroach	0	
	Pueraria montana	Encroach	0	
	Pyrus calleryana	Encroach	0	
	Ranunculus ficaria	Encroach	0	
	Sorghum halepense	Encroach	0	
	Trapa natans	Encroach	0	
	Viburnum dilatatum	Encroach	0	

probable locations of these species and could be used to guide targeted search efforts for new or previously unknown infestations. However, the species in this scenario have minimal occurrences and the data may not reflect the full range of environmental settings in which the species could thrive. Therefore, the model results could be strongly influenced by the environmental factors at the small number of known locations.

Scenario C represents species that were not found during sampling efforts but are serious threats to high-priority resources in the park. The models would create potential distribution maps that would provide probable locations of these species and could be used to guide targeted search efforts for new or previously unknown infestations. The results may also provide information on the extent of the threat posed by this species. However, the major caveat is that there are no known locations for these species within the park. Therefore, models will be based on professional expertise of species habitat constraints and preferences instead of statistical correlations between known locations and environmental factors.

From this process, 11 species and one vegetation community type were selected for parkwide predictive modeling and are described in detail in the Study Species section.

Environmental Variables

Environmental variables were chosen based on the potential contribution to invasive exotic species' distributions (Table 2). All environmental data was converted into 10-meter resolution ASCII and GRID files using geographic information systems (GIS) software (ArcGIS 9.2, ESRI) and clipped to the extent of the park boundary.

Topographic surface variables were derived to characterize habitat. Slope, aspect, and terrain shape index (TSI) were derived from the 10-m digital elevation models (DEM) (USGS) in ArcGIS using the Slope, Aspect, and Math Algebra tools under the Spatial Analyst extension. Aspect was transformed into a solar radiation index using a modified version of Beers et al. (1966) aspect transformation (TransAsp = ((- cos (45 – aspect)) +1) × 100) using the Math Algebra tool. The modified version produces an index ranging from 0–200 with northeast facing aspects equaling 0 and southwestern facing aspects equaling 200. Terrain shape index is a measure of the surface shape of a pixel (concave or convex), correlating to landscape features such as ridges or valleys (McNab 1989) (TSI = DEM – focalmean (DEM, circle, radius (10))). The index ranges from a negative number (convex/valley) to a positive number (concave/ridge).

Community vegetation data was used to address specific habitat associations that species may prefer. Community vegetation mapping had been completed for the park in 2006 by the Pennsylvania Natural Heritage Program (Perles et al. 2007; Perles et al. in review). The vegetation dataset consisted of spatially delineated boundaries for natural communities so that specific vegetation communities were assigned to specific polygons. DEWA contained a total of 4,987 polygons representing 69 vegetation community types and UPDE contained a total of 3,527 polygons representing 48 vegetation community types.

Soil property variables were derived from digital soil survey data (Soil Conservation Service, USDA). Soil drainage capacity was classified into seven classes: excessively drained; somewhat excessively drained; well drained; moderately well drained; somewhat poorly drained; poorly drained; and very poorly drained. A soil pH layer was also derived from the soil data and kept in continuous format.

Variables contributing to light availability, such as canopy cover and area of edge influence, were derived. Canopy cover was derived from aerial interpretation in the vegetation mapping process for each community type. Canopy cover was classified into four classes: 0–25%; 25–50%; 50–75%; and 75–100%. Area of edge influence was derived using vegetation community, transportation (PA DOT and digitized from aerial imagery) and hydrologic layers (derived from vegetation mapping layer). A buffer distance of 30 m (98.4 ft) was applied to features that create habitat edges such as roads, streams, rivers, and open canopy vegetation communities. The 30-m distance was the distance where environmental variables varied significantly from forest edges in a New Jersey deciduous forest (Meiners and Pickett 1999) and approximately the mean distance of edge influence reported for regenerating and maintained eastern North American forests (Harper et al. 2005). Road widths were taken into account during the buffering process.

Table 2. Environmental variables used to model invasive plant species distributions in Delaware Water Gap National Recreation Area. This table provides a brief description of the variable, its data source, and the variable's abbreviation when used in analyses.

Predictor Category	Environmental Variable	Description	Data Source	Abbreviation for Analyses
Topographic	Slope	Percent slope. Slope is indirectly related to soil moisture and soil erosion.	Slope tool in ArcGIS	slope
	Transformed aspect	A solaration index based on aspect. This variable is indirectly related to soil moisture.	$((- \cos (45 - aspect)) +1) \times 100)$	trans_asp
	Terrain Shape Index (TSI)	A topographic position index.	DEM – focalmean (DEM, circle, radius (10))	tsi
Soil properties	Soil drainage	Drainage class of a soil in terms of its capability to retain water.	USDA Soil Survey	drainage
	Soil pH	Soil pH is related to nutrient uptake and solubility.	USDA Soil Survey	soil_ph
Vegetation	Vegetation	Delineated vegetation community types.	National Park Service vegetation map of the parks	veg_com
Light availability	Canopy cover	Percent canopy cover for vegetation communities within the park.	National Park Service vegetation map of the parks	can_cov
	Edge effects	Area of edge influence resulting from fragmenting features. Variable identifies areas of light penetration in intact communities.	National Park Service vegetation map of the parks	edge_eff

Additionally any community polygons that had canopy cover classes lower then 50% were treated as fragmenting features given their open canopies. Such polygons were buffered and included in this layer. Ponds and streams were then removed from the layer although any area of edge effects resulting from them was left intact.

Study Species

<u>Scenario A</u>

Japanese barberry (*Berberis thunbergii* DC. [photographs of all study species are in Appendix A]) is an exotic ornamental shrub that escaped cultivation and can invade open areas as well as relatively undisturbed closed canopy forests (Ehrenfeld 1997; Silander and Klepeis 1999). *B. thunbergii* can tolerate a wide range of light conditions and can produce fruit at light levels less than 4% (Silander and Klepeis 1999). Studies suggest that the species may be nitrogen limited (Cassidy et al. 2004; Harrington et al. 2004). Increased pH, nitrogen availabilit, and exotic earthworm abundance have been documented under *B. thunbergii* plants compared to soil conditions under native shrubs (Kourtev et al. 1999). Such alterations to the soil conditions may displace native plant species and promote future invasions of exotic plants (Kourtev et al. 1999).

Tree-of-heaven (*Ailanthus altissima* ([Mill.] Swingle) is an exotic tree species that is native to Asia and is typically found in open disturbed areas (Rhoads and Block 2007) and forest canopy gaps. In open disturbed areas, *A. altissima* may benefit from increased mycorrhizal colonization when compared to plants in forested areas, possibly allowing the plant to utilize resources more efficiently in a stressful environment (Huebner et al. 2007). In forested areas, the species has been shown to exhibit high seedling mortality and therefore relies on vegetative reproduction, forming dense clonal patches (Kowarik 1995), until forest gaps provide the light resources needed for canopy growth (Kowarik 1995; Knapp and Canham 2000). Additionally, the species produces allelopathic compounds that suppress surrounding plant species (Lawerence et al. 1991).

Spotted knapweed (*Centaurea biebersteinii* DC.) is an exotic species native to Europe that invades open disturbed habitats (Watson and Renny 1974) such as dry woods, fields, roadsides, and shale barrens (Rhoads and Block 2007). Seed germination can occur in closed canopies (Spears et al. 1980); however, mature plants are uncommon in lower light conditions (Watson and Renny 1974). Seeds may last several years within the seed bank resulting in long persistent populations (Davis et al. 1993). *C. biebersteinii* produces allelopathic compounds which, in combination with resource competition, may displace native vegetation (Locken and Kelsey 1987).

Winged euonymus (*Euonymus alatus* [Thunb.] Siebold) is an exotic shrub native to Asia. *E. alatus* tends to occur in mesic forests as well as disturbed habitats (Searcy et al. 2006; Rhoads and Block 2007), but persists in a range of soil types and light conditions (Mehrhoff et al. 2003). The species can form dense thickets that often outshade native vegetation.

Common mullein (*Verbascum thapsus* L.) is an exotic species that is native to Eurasia and grows in open disturbed areas (Reinartz 1984). The species tends to prefer dry, sandy, rocky, or highly calcareous soils (Reinartz 1984). Full sunlight is required for seed germination (Semenza et al. 1978) and seeds germinate only on bare soil (Gross and Werner 1982). Populations are long persistent due to a large seed source, as seeds are viable in seed banks for up to 100 years (Kivilaan and Bandurski 1973; Gross and Werner 1982).

Common reed (*Phragmites australis* [Cav.] Trin ex Steud.) is a gramanoid species believed to consist of many native and nonnative genetic strains. In general, the rapidly expanding populations are believed to be of exotic origin and slower spreading populations are native (Hauber et al. 1991). A major concern is the species' ability to utilize lower marshes originally thought to be unsuitable habitat, as well as its expansion into wetlands (Amsberry et al. 2000). As a result, the species alters important habitat for fauna. *P. australis* tends to prefer marshes and disturbed mesic habitats, including roadsides (Rhoads and Block 2007).

Scenario B

Norway maple (*Acer platanoides* L.) is a native to Europe and frequents roadsides, disturbed areas, and closed canopied forests in its nonnative range (Kloeppel and Abrams 1995). *A. platanoides* is shade-tolerant and forms dense crown cover as well as shallow root systems (Wyckoff and Webb 1996). The species undergoes early leaf expansion and experiences a longer growing season in comparison to surrounding native tree species (Kloeppel and Abrams 1995). Such traits may give the species a competitive advantage over native species. For example, studies indicate *A. platanoides* may suppress native understory vegetation (Wyckoff and Webb 1996) and sugar maple (*Acer saccharum* L.) regeneration (Kloeppel and Abrams 1995; Webb et al. 2001).

Mile-a-minute (*Polygonum perfoliatum* L.) is an exotic vine native to Asia (Rhoads and Block 2007). *P. perfoliatum* grows predominantly in disturbed sites, such as roadsides, forest edges, and agricultural fields, but can also be found in open mesic natural areas (Oliver 1996). The species appears to have a preference for mesic soil conditions (Riefner and Windler 1979) and medium to high light availability (Mountain 1989; Kumar and DiTommaso 2005); however, the species has been documented to occur in shade and in dry or wet conditions (Kumar and DiTommaso 2005). *P. perfoliatum* forms dense canopy-like mats that outshade and limit growth of native species underneath (Oliver 1996).

Scenario C

Narrowleaf bittercress (*Cardamine impatiens* L.) is an herbaceous plant that is native to Europe. The species is found in moist woods and disturbed areas (USDA 2002; Rhoads and Block 2007) and prefers shaded mesic habitats (Cusick 1993). *C. impatiens* has the potential to form dense carpets of vegetation and outcompete native vegetation (USDA 2002).

Japanese hops (*Humulus japonicus* Sieb. & Zucc.) is an exotic vine native to Asia. This species tends to inhabit mesic open fields and disturbed areas as well as floodplain areas (Mehrhoff et al. 2003; Rhoads and Block 2007). *H. japonicus* outcompetes native species by forming dense mats and preventing sunlight penetration to species underneath (Mehrhoff et al. 2003).

Fig buttercup (*Ranunculus ficaria* L.) is an herbaceous plant that is native to Europe. *R. ficaria* tends to prefer high light conditions and mesic habitat such as open woods, floodplains, meadows, and disturbed areas (Mehrhoff et al. 2003; Rhoads and Block 2007). The species emerges before native spring ephemerals and outcompetes native vegetation by forming dense mats (Mehrhoff et al. 2003).

11

Communities

Eastern hemlock (*Tsuga canadensis* L.) communities are subject to invasion by exotic invasive plant species through hemlock woolly adelgid (*Adelgis tsugae*) infestations. Native to Japan, *A. tsugae* feeds on the twigs of the eastern hemlocks causing defoliation, bud mortality, and, eventually, tree mortality, typically within as little as four years (Young et al. 1995). As tree mortality occurs, light availability increases due to the widening of canopy gaps. As a result, invasive species are typically able to colonize the understory and invade the susceptible stands (Orwig and Foster 1998). Park biologists are interested in identifying eastern hemlock communities that are susceptible to invasion by exotic species as defoliation and eastern hemlock mortality occurs.

Modeling Approaches – Invasive Species Distributions

Data was pooled for both DEWA and UPDE to increase sample sizes for species. Only sample points that had an abundance of occasional or abundant percent cover were used for this analysis in order to preserve data accuracy. For example, the rare category only represents a small percent cover in a relatively large plot size and the probability of the species occurring at the center point of the plot (the spatial sample unit) would be low compared to the occasional and abundant categories. CART and logistic regression models were initially built for *Ailanthus altissima* and *Berberis thunbergii*; however, such models contained minimal splits and, as a result, were found to be extremely generalized for the project's goals. Due to the ability of maximum entropy modeling in handling low sample sizes, maximum entropy models using the Maxent software program (Maxent 3.2.1, Princeton University) were built for species within Scenario A as well as for *Polygonum perfoliatum* and *Humulus japonicus*. Environmental variables were extracted to species occurrence locations using GIS software (ArcGIS 9.2, ESRI [GIS deliverables are in Appendix B]). A correlation matrix was used to test for co-linearity between environmental variables for each species using Minitab v. 15, Minitab Inc. If variables were correlated ($p < 0.05$) and had a Pearson's correlation value greater then 0.700, variables were reduced to avoid multi-collinearity and over-fitting of the model. However, none of the variables were correlated and all variables were included for modeling purposes. Twenty-five percent of the occurrence data was randomly withheld for each species as an evaluation dataset to test model validity. Additionally, Maxent runs a jackknife test of variable importance measure to test for information gain of environmental variables. This approach builds models solely on each environmental variable as well as models without the target variable in order to quantify the amount of information contained in such variable. Variables are weighted based on their importance values during the construction of the final model.

Predicted suitable habitat was discriminated from unsuitable habitat based on threshold values. A threshold value serves as a cut off point to distinguish between predicted presence and absence. Selecting maximum entropy threshold values for assessing a model's predictions are a topic that is of current debate. A general rule is that commission errors (false positives) decrease and omission errors (false negatives) increase when larger threshold values are applied to the model (Fielding and Bell 1997; Hernandez et al. 2006). In modeling approaches, sensitivity is defined as the percentage of true positives correctly predicted (100% - commission error) and specificity is defined as the percentage of true negatives correctly predicted (100% - omission error). If there is no preference for minimizing either commission or omission rates in the model, threshold values which incorporate the maximum sensitivity and specificity value of the data can be used (Manel et al. 2001). Considering the nature of the study, this approach was taken and the maximum sensitivity and specificity value for either the modeling or evaluation data was used to produce binary predicted presence/absence maps (Hernandez et al. 2006). Therefore, pixels with predicted probabilities greater than the threshold value were considered suitable habitat and pixels with lower probabilities were considered unsuitable habitat. To fully evaluate each model's performance, 1,000 randomly sampled points containing absence data from the vegetation mapping efforts were compared to the distribution maps to identify false negatives.

Heuristic models were built for *Acer platanoides*, *Cardamine impatiens*, and *Ranunculus ficaria* due to excessively small sample sizes. The models were built based upon the species' habitat preferences derived from scientific literature (see Study Species section). All data layers were overlaid in GIS and suitable habitat was delineated where all the parameters overlapped. In order to fully evaluate the model's performance for each species, any known presence points and 1,000 randomly sampled points containing absence data from the vegetation mapping efforts were used. Table 3 lists samples sizes and environmental variable parameters used to model species distributions.

Model accuracy was calculated for both the model (training) and evaluation (testing) datasets based on the overall accuracy (percentage of correctly predicted known presence and absence points), error of commission (percentage of false positives), error of omissions (percentage of false negatives), and the True Skill Statistic (TSS). TSS is an index that compares the observed agreement against what is expected by chance. This measure measures from 1.0 (perfect agreement) to -1.0 (complete disagreement). Maximum entropy uses only presence data and pseudo-absences, randomly sampled background data treated as an absence dataset. Therefore, error of commission for the modeling dataset cannot be calculated. Heuristic models lack a modeling dataset and were only evaluated on the evaluation data.

Modeling Approaches – Plant Community Invasibility

Eastern hemlock (*Tsuga canadensis*) communities were ranked using a landscape metric designed to predict the susceptibility of the stand to being invaded by exotic plant species. This metric incorporates canopy gaps and area of edge influence, as well as the number and abundance of invasive plant species within hemlock stands and their adjacent forest stands. Polygons identified in the park's vegetation association map as Eastern Hemlock Forest, Dry Eastern Hemlock - Oak Forest, Eastern Hemlock - Northern Hardwood Forest, and Eastern Hemlock - Mixed Hardwood Palustrine Forest were considered "eastern hemlock communities" for this analysis. Community scores were developed in order to quantify the amount of degradation within that community polygon. All community polygons within the park boundaries were given a categorical score for percent canopy cover, percent edge, invasive species abundance, and number of invasive species, so that each category score ranged from zero to four (Table 4). If the community did not have a sampling point recorded for invasive species

Table 3. Species sample sizes for both the modeling and evaluation dataset and predictors used to model species distributions. Samples sizes indicate the number of presence (excluding the rare category points) and absence points used for the respective species.

Modeling Method	Species	Modeling Dataset	Evaluation Dataset	Predictors
Maximum Entropy	*Ailanthus altissima*	111 present	36 present 1,000 absent	All variables.
	Berberis thunbergii	111 present	36 present 1,000 absent	All variables.
	Centaurea biebersteinii	22 present	7 present 1,000 absent	All variables.
	Euonymus alatus	18 present	5 present 1,000 absent	All variables.
	Humulus japonicus	10 present	3 present 1,000 absent	All variables
	Phragmites australis	16 present	5 present 1,000 absent	All variables.
	Polygonum perfoliatum	4 present	1 present 1,000 absent	All variables
	Verbascum thapsus	15 present	4 present 1,000 absent	All variables.
Heuristic	*Acer platanoides*	-	3 present 1,000 absent	Drainage (well drained, moderately well drained and somewhat poorly drained), edge effects, vegetation (successional, riparian and mesic terrestrial communities)
	Cardamine impatiens	-	0 present 1,000 absent	Cover (25–100%), drainage (well drained, moderately well drained and somewhat poorly drained), edge effects, vegetation (successional, riparian, mesic terrestrial and palustrine communities)
	Ranunculus ficaria	-	0 present 1,000 absent	Cover (0–50%), drainage (well drained, moderately well drained and somewhat poorly drained), edge effects, vegetation (successional, riparian, mesic terrestrial and palustrine communities)

Table 4. Community score criteria and subsequent ranking of category scores.

Community Score Criteria	Criteria Source	Criteria Value	Category Score
% canopy cover	Canopy cover class derived from vegetation mapping efforts performed by Pennsylvania Natural Heritage Program	100–75%	1
		75–50%	2
		50–25%	3
		0–25%	4
% edge	Amount of edge effects layer that intersects community	0%	0
		0–25%	1
		25–50%	2
		50–75%	3
		75–100%	4
Invasive species abundance	Total abundance (cover) of invasive species per sampling point based upon accuracy assessment points within community polygon	0	0
		0–25	1
		25–50	2
		50–75	3
		75+	4
Number of invasive species	Number of invasive species per sampling point based upon accuracy assessment points within community polygon	0	0
		1–2	1
		2–5	2
		5–8	3
		8+	4

only the percent canopy cover and percent edge were averaged to formulate the community score below. Based on these criteria, an overall community score was derived from the following formula:

Community Score = ([Cover Score + Edge Score + Abundance Score + Species Score] / 4).

The resulting score ranged in value from 0.0–4.0 with a value of 0.0 representing conditions that are least likely to be invaded and a value of 4.0 indicating areas of high susceptibility to invasion.

With communities scores developed, we felt it was important to emphasize the influence of surrounding communities on the dispersal and flux of invasive species into the hemlock communities. To account for this, scores for community polygons directly adjacent to hemlock communities were weighted based upon the proportion of shared perimeter to the hemlock polygon and then averaged. This score was then averaged with the hemlock community polygon's score to produce an index of susceptibility to invasion:

$$\text{Index}_{\text{hemlock}} = ([\text{Avg. Community Score}_{\text{adjacent comm.}} + \text{Community Score}_{\text{eastern hemlock comm}}] / 2)$$

Averaging the mean scores for adjacent communities with the hemlock community scores placed an emphasis on inter- and intra-community dynamics. The final index of susceptibility to invasion for hemlock communities ranges from 0.0–4.0 with 0.0 being least likely to be invaded.

To further understand current invasive species' distributions, all vegetation communities were ranked based on an infestation index to derive areas of high and low invasive activity. Vegetation community polygons (n=1,204) were given an infestation value based on the abundance per sampling point and species per sampling point rank values derived in the eastern hemlock community analysis. The abundance and species ranks were averaged to give an infestation index using the following formula:

Infestation Index = ([Abundance Score + Species Score] / 2).

Only community polygons containing sampled accuracy assessment points were included in this analysis to maintain data accuracy. The index ranges from 0.0–4.0 with a value of 0.0 representing areas of no invasion and a value of 4.0 representing highly infested communities. The resulting index is indicative of the community's current invasion status. Rare communities were addressed in this analysis to identify areas where park managers may wish to concentrate invasive species management efforts.

Current Status and Distribution of Invasive Plant Species

Based on the results of the accuracy assessment survey, no changes in the status of the target invasive species occurrence within the park are proposed. Of the 44 species labeled as Present, 36 were observed and 8 were not observed in this study. None of the 16 species labeled Encroaching were observed in this study. The one species labeled Unconfirmed was also not observed in this study.

Although invasive plant species are abundant in some areas of the park, invasive plants are not currently ubiquitous. Approximately 34% of the sampling points were free of invasive species and 17% of the sampling points contained only one invasive species (Table 5). Unfortunately, 49% of the sampling points contained two or more invasive species. One sampling point that occurred in a Silky Dogwood Successional Palustrine Shrubland contained 10 invasive species.

The observed distributions and abundances varied widely among species (Table 6). Some species were widespread, while others had limited distribution. The top ten most abundant species (labeled Top 10 Worst Offenders in Table 6) are clearly more widespread than the other target species. Without biological control, it is unlikely that these species can be contained or controlled. However, at specific high-priority sites that are not already heavily invaded by these species, it may be possible to prevent the colonization of invasive species by using persistent management.

Table 5. Number of invasive species observed at each sampling point in the Delaware Water Gap National Recreation Area.

Number of Invasive Species Observed at Point	Number of Data Points	Percent of Data Points
0	455	33.6%
1	229	16.9%
2	191	14.1%
3	180	13.3%
4	147	10.8%
5	74	5.5%
6	50	3.7%
7	18	1.3%
8	6	0.4%
9	4	0.3%
10	1	0.1%
Total	1,355	100.0%

Table 6. Abundance, frequency, and number of vegetation associations that contained target invasive species in the Delaware Water Gap National Recreation Area. Total abundance is the sum of the abundances for all sampling points the species was observed. Total frequency is the sum of all sampling points the species was observed.

Scientific Name	Status	Total Abundance	Number of Sampling Points which Species was Present	Number of Vegetation Associations	Top 10 Worst Offenders
Microstegium vimineum	Present	13,242	369	59	X
Rosa multiflora	Present	10,772	432	60	X
Berberis thunbergii	Present	9,432	467	53	X
Alliaria petiolata	Present	9,111	357	55	X
Lonicera morrowii	Present	5,060	193	43	X
Elaeagnus umbellata	Present	4,765	184	40	X
Polygonum cuspidatum	Present	3,203	73	20	X
Lythrum salicaria	Present	2,452	91	31	X
Celastrus orbiculatus	Present	1,956	95	35	X
Ailanthus altissima	Present	1,448	62	26	X
Phragmites australis	Present	721	18	9	
Lonicera japonica	Present	674	31	19	
Rubus phoenicolasius	Present	668	39	24	
Euonymus alatus	Present	565	31	22	
Centaurea biebersteinii	Present	545	34	16	
Vinca minor	Present	510	11	8	
Coronilla varia	Present	290	9	6	
Lonicera maackii	Present	262	8	7	
Elaeagnus angustifolia	Present	211	12	9	
Wisteria sinensis	Present	210	6	6	
Hesperis matronalis	Present	167	18	12	
Lonicera tatarica	Present	145	9	6	
Ligustrum sp.	Present	120	21	12	
Verbascum thapsus	Present	112	31	19	
Acer platanoides	Present	80	3	3	
Carduus nutans	Present	80	3	3	
Tussilago farfara	Present	70	2	2	
Rhamnus cathartica	Present	64	5	3	
Paulownia tomentosa	Present	61	2	2	
Myriophyllum spicatum	Present	60	1	1	
Cirsium arvense	Present	30	3	2	
Eupatorium serotinum	Present	13	4	4	
Polygonum perfoliatum	Present	11	2	2	
Akebia quinata	Present	10	1	1	
Polygonum sachalinense	Present	10	1	1	
Lychnis flos-cuculi	Present	1	1	1	
Acer palmatum	Present	0	0	0	
Albizia julibrissin	Present	0	0	0	
Anthriscus sylvestris	Present	0	0	0	
Cabomba caroliniana	Present	0	0	0	

Table 6. Abundance, frequency, and number of vegetation associations that contained target invasive species in the Delaware Water Gap National Recreation Area (continued). Total abundance is the sum of the abundances for all sampling points the species was observed. Total frequency is the sum of all sampling points the species was observed.

Scientific Name	Status	Total Abundance	Number of Sampling Points which Species was Present	Number of Vegetation Associations	Top 10 Worst Offenders
Hedera helix	Present	0	0	0	
Lespedeza cuneata	Present	0	0	0	
Potamogeton crispus	Present	0	0	0	
Wisteria floribunda	Present	0	0	0	
Myriophyllum heterophyllum	Unconfirmed	0	0	0	
Ampelopsis brevipedunculata	Encroach	0	0	0	
Cardamine impatiens	Encroach	0	0	0	
Cynanchum louiseae	Encroach	0	0	0	
Cynanchum rossicum	Encroach	0	0	0	
Egeria densa	Encroach	0	0	0	
Frangula alnus	Encroach	0	0	0	
Heracleum mantegazzianum	Encroach	0	0	0	
Humulus japonicus	Encroach	0	0	0	
Hydrilla verticillata	Encroach	0	0	0	
Phellodendron japonicum	Encroach	0	0	0	
Pueraria montana	Encroach	0	0	0	
Pyrus calleryana	Encroach	0	0	0	
Ranunculus ficaria	Encroach	0	0	0	
Sorghum halepense	Encroach	0	0	0	
Trapa natans	Encroach	0	0	0	
Viburnum dilatatum	Encroach	0	0	0	

Most invasive species thrive in a wide variety of environmental settings. However, our data confirmed that even obnoxious invasive species have habitat preferences and constraints. Among the Top 10 Worst Offender species, four species showed affinities to certain vegetation associations. Thus, the vegetation associations listed below are likely particularly susceptible to the following invasive species:

Ailanthus altissima

Eastern Red-cedar (Pitch Pine) - Prickly Pear Shale Woodland, Shale Scree Slope, and Sparsely Vegetated Sandstone Cliff.

Elaeagnus umbellata

Abundant in Eastern Red-cedar Forest, Old Field, Successional Shrubland, and Silky Dogwood Successional Palustrine Shrubland. Frequent at low abundance in Little Bluestem Grassland.

Lythrum salicaria

Open palustrine and riparian associations such as Riverine Scour Vegetation, Calcareous Riverside Outcrop / Calcareous Riverside Seep, Sycamore - Mixed Hardwood Riverine Shrubland, Tussock Sedge Marsh, Silky Dogwood Successional Palustrine Shrubland, Alder Wetland, Calcareous Fen, Marl Seep Fen, Wet Meadow, and Mixed Forb Marsh.

Polygonum cuspidatum

Riparian associations such as Riverine Scour Vegetation, Reed Canary Grass Riverine Grassland, Big Bluestem - Indian Grass River Grassland, Calcareous Riverside Outcrop / Calcareous Riverside Seep, Sycamore (Willow) - Mixed Hardwood Riverine Dwarf Shrubland, Sycamore - Mixed Hardwood Riverine Shrubland, Sycamore Floodplain Forest, Sycamore - Mixed Hardwood Floodplain Forest, Silver Maple Floodplain Forest, and Bitternut Hickory Lowland Forest.

Model Accuracy

Table 7 provides a summary of measures of model accuracy for invasive species distribution models. There are several considerations that need to be addressed when interpreting the model accuracy results. High testing omission and commission rates are indicative of a model that overfit the modeling dataset and therefore does not perform well when cross validated with the evaluation dataset. In turn, an overfit model usually results in a low TSS value. Overall accuracy only considers the amount of correctly predicted presences and absences and may not be the best measure of model accuracy, since it does not consider the proportional contribution of the evaluation dataset when the sample sizes are not equal for known presences and absences. TSS provides a more robust measurement by offsetting the bias from overall accuracy by taking into account the sample sizes for known presences (prevalence) (Alouche et al. 2006).

Table 7. Measures of model accuracy for invasive species distribution models.

Species	Threshold Value (%)	Area Predicted (hectares)	Training Omission Error (%)	Test Omission Error (%)	Test Commission Error (%)	Overall Accuracy (%)	TSS
A. platanoides	-	4,577.2	-	66.7	14.8	85.1	0.185
A. altissima	24.2	5,572.6	6.3	13.9	13.3	86.4	0.728
B. thunbergii	32.4	9,742.0	7.2	25.0	27.8	74.0	0.438
C. impatiens	-	2,068.0	-	-	10.2	89.8	-
C. biebersteinii	22.0	1,903.8	0.0	28.6	9.0	91.1	0.624
E. alatus	14.2	8,890.0	0.0	40.0	28.4	72.0	0.316
H. japonicus	19.5	1,130.2	0.0	0.0	11.1	89.0	0.889
P. australis	25.3	778.3	0.0	0.0	7.9	92.3	0.921
P. perfoliatum	28.4	1,184.9	0.0	0.0	7.3	92.7	0.927
R. ficaria	-	2,850.7	-	-	10.3	89.7	-
V. thapsus	22.1	2,950.3	0.0	0.0	16.0	71.9	0.519

Maximum Entropy Models

Jackknife tests of training gain are used to evaluate the amount of information each environmental variable contributes to the predictive distribution model. Maximum entropy modeling builds several hundred iterations of models using every combination of environmental variables. The models are then compared to see which environmental variable contains the most information when added to or subtracted from the models.

The predicted distribution of tree-of-heaven (*Ailanthus altissima*) was 5,572.6 ha (13,770.1 ac), or 20.0% of the total park area. The model had a training omission of 6.3%, test omission of 13.9%, test commission of 13.3%, overall accuracy of 86.4%, and TSS of 0.728. Vegetation community, edge effects, soil pH, and canopy cover have the highest variable importance on the species' predicted distribution (Figure 1 [due to physical [page] size, Table 9 and Figures 1–22 are grouped together at the end of the Results section]). The species was predicted to occur most frequently in Cropland, Northeastern Modified Successional Forests, Successional Shrublands, Old Fields, Dry Oak - Mixed Hardwood Forests, and Red Maple - Sweet Birch Hardwood Forests. Probability of occurrence for *A. altissima* also tended to peak between soil pH values of 5.2 and 6.5. The model predicts the species to occur most frequently in 0–25% canopy cover, followed by 50–75% and 75%–100% canopy cover. However, the latter two classes were almost predominately within the area of edge influence. Figure 2 depicts the predicted suitable habitat for this species.

The predicted distribution of Japanese barberry (*Berberis thunbergii*) was 9,742.0 ha (24,072.9 ac), or 34.9% of the total park area. The model had a training omission of 7.2%, test omission of 25.0%, test commission of 27.8%, overall accuracy of 74.0%, and TSS of 0.438. Vegetation community, soil pH, and canopy cover have the highest variable importance on the species' predicted distribution (Figure 3). The species was predicted to occur most frequently in Northeastern Modified Successional Forests, Sugar Maple - American Beech - Sweet Birch Forests, Red Maple - Sweet Birch Hardwood Forests, Northern Red Oak - Mixed Hardwood Forest, Eastern White Pine - Successional Hardwood Forests, Successional Shrublands, Conifer Plantations, and Silver Maple Floodplain Forests. Probability of occurrence tends to be highest near soil pH values of 6.5 to 7.2 and under canopy covers of 50–100%. Figure 4 depicts the predicted suitable habitat for this species.

The predicted distribution of spotted knapweed (*Centaurea biebersteinii*) was 1,903.8 ha (4,704.4 ac), or 6.8% of the total park area. The model had a training omission of 0.0%, test omission of 28.6%, test commission of 9.0%, overall accuracy of 91.1%, and TSS of 0.624. Vegetation community, canopy cover, and edge effects have the highest variable importance on the species' predicted distribution (Figure 5). The species was predicted to occur most frequently in Successional Shrublands, Old Fields, Successional Bear Oak - Heath Shrublands, and Dry Eastern White Pine - Oak Forests, and mostly under 0–25% canopy cover. It was also predicted to occur under 25–100% canopy cover; however, almost all of these predicted areas were in the area of edge influence. Figure 6 depicts the predicted suitable habitat for this species.

The predicted distribution of winged euonymus (*Euonymus alatus*) was 8,890.0 ha (21,967.6 ac), or 31.8% of the total park area. The model had a training omission of 0.0%, test omission of

40.0%, test commission of 28.4%, overall accuracy of 72.0%, and TSS of 0.316. Vegetation community, canopy cover, and edge effects have the highest variable importance on the species' predicted distribution (Figure 7). The species was predicted to occur most frequently in Sugar Maple - American Beech - Sweet Birch Forests, Northeastern Modified Successional Forests, Red Maple - Sweet Birch Hardwood Forests, Dry Eastern White Pine - Oak Forests, Cropland, Successional Shrublands, Eastern White Pine - Successional Hardwood Forests, and Eastern Hemlock - Northern Hardwood Forests. The species is predominately predicted to occur either in or out of the area of edge influence for 75–100% canopy cover class as well as in the 0–25% canopy cover class. Figure 8 depicts the predicted suitable habitat for this species.

The predicted distribution of Japanese hops (*Humulus japonicus*) was 1,130.2 ha (2,792.8 ac), or 4.0% of the total park area. The model had a training omission of 0.0%, test omission of 0.0%, test commission of 11.1%, overall accuracy of 89.0%, and TSS of 0.889. Vegetation community, canopy cover, and edge effects have the highest variable importance on the species' predicted distribution (Figure 9). The species was predicted to occur most frequently in Silver Maple Floodplain Forests, Ponds, Successional Shrublands, Croplands, and Sycamore - Mixed Hardwood Floodplain Forests. The species was predominately predicted to occur in 0–25% and 50–75% canopy cover classes within the area of edge influence. Figure 10 depicts the predicted suitable habitat for this species.

The predicted distribution of common reed (*Phragmites australis*) was 778.3 ha (1,923.2 ac), or 2.8% of the total park area. The model had a training omission of 0.0%, test omission of 0.0%, test commission of 7.9%, overall accuracy of 92.3%, and TSS of 0.921. Vegetation community type, canopy cover, edge effects, and soil drainage class have the highest variable importance on the species' predicted distribution (Figure 11). The species was predicted to occur most frequently in Successional Shrublands, Ponds, Wet Meadows, and Silky Dogwood Successional Palustrine Shrublands. The species was predominately predicted to occur on well drained and very poorly drained soil drainage classes within the 0–25% canopy cover class. Figure 12 depicts the predicted suitable habitat for this species.

The predicted distribution of mile-a-minute weed (*Polygonum perfoliatum*) was 1,148.9 ha (2,838.9 ac), or 4.2% of the total park area. The model had a training omission of 0.0%, test omission of 0.0%, test commission of 7.3%, overall accuracy of 92.7%, and TSS of 0.927. Vegetation community, slope, soil drainage class, and canopy cover have the highest variable importance on the species' predicted distribution (Figure 13). The species was predicted to occur most frequently in Northeastern Modified Successional Forests, Ponds, Dry Oak - Heath Forests, Silver Maple Floodplain Forests, and Bottomland Mixed Hardwood Palustrine Forests. The species was predominately predicted to occur on well drained and somewhat excessively drained soil drainage classes within the 50–75% and 0–25% canopycover classes on little or no slope. Figure 14 depicts the predicted suitable habitat for this species.

The predicted distribution of common mullein (*Verbascum thapsus*) was 2,950.3 ha (7,290.3 ac), or 10.6% of the total park area. The model had a training omission of 0.0%, test omission of 0.0%, test commission of 16.0%, overall accuracy of 84.0%, and TSS of 0.84. Vegetation community, canopy cover, and edge effects have the highest variable importance on the species' predicted distribution (Figure 15). The species was predicted to occur most frequently in Successional Shrublands, Croplands, Northern Red Oak - Mixed Hardwood Forests, and

Northeastern Modified Successional Forests. The species was predominately predicted to occur within 0–25% canopy cover classes and within the area of edge influence. Figure 16 depicts the predicted suitable habitat for this species.

Heuristic Models

The potential distribution of Norway maple (*Acer platanoides*) was 4,577.2 ha (11,310.5 ac), or 16.4% of the total park area. The model had a test omission of 66.7%, test commission of 13.3%, and overall accuracy of 85.1%. The model predicted *A. platanoides* to occur most frequently in Croplands, Successional Shrublands, Northeastern Modified Successional Forests, Old Fields, Built-Up Lands, and Sugar Maple - American Beech - Sweet Birch Forests. Figure 17 depicts the predicted suitable habitat for this species.

The potential distribution of narrowleaf bittercress (*Cardamine impatiens*) was 2068.0 ha (5,110.1 ac), or 7.4% of the total park area. The model had a test commission of 10.2% and overall accuracy of 89.8%. The model predicted *C. impatiens* to occur most frequently under 50–100% canopy cover in Northeastern Modified Successional Forests, Sugar Maple - American Beech - Sweet Birch Forests, Red Maple - Sweet Birch Hardwood Forests, Silver Maple Floodplain Forests and Northern Red Oak - Mixed Hardwood Forests. Figure 18 depicts the predicted suitable habitat for this species.

The potential distribution of fig buttercup (*Ranunculus ficaria*) was predicted to occur in 2850.7 ha (7,044.2 ac), or 10.2% of the total park area. The model had a test omission of 25.0%, test commission of 10.3%, and overall accuracy of 89.7%. The model predicted *R. ficaria* to occur most frequently under 0–25% canopy cover in Croplands, Successional Shrublands, Old Fields, Built-Up Lands, and Transportation Corridors. Figure 19 depicts the predicted suitable habitat for this species.

All predictive models were combined to show areas which could be deemed hotspots for invasions by exotic plant species (Figure 20). Collectively, the models predicted 11,430.7 ha (28,245.7 ac [41.0% of the total park area]) to contain no overlap among invasive species distributions and 3.0 ha (7.4 ac [0.0% of the total park area]) for overlap between nine of the modeled species (Table 8). Additionally, the models predicted only 20.7% of the park to contain three or more of the species modeled.

Community Models

Eastern hemlock (*Tsuga canadensis*) communities ranged in values in terms of susceptibility to invasion. The analysis identified 1 minimally susceptible (index value of 0), 217 slightly susceptible (index value of 1), 83 moderately susceptible (index value of 2), 16 moderate to highly susceptible (index value of 3), and no highly susceptible polygons of *T. canadensis* communities (index value of 4). Minimally susceptible communities had a total area of 3.9 ha (9.6 ac [0.1%] of total eastern hemlock community area). Slightly susceptible communities had a total area of 2,699.0 ha (6,669.3 ac [83.4%] of total eastern hemlock community area). Moderately susceptible communities had a total area of 493.7 ha (1219.9 ac [15.3%] of total hemlock community area). Moderate to highly susceptible areas had a total of 40.2 ha (99.3 ac

Table 8. Area predicted for combined invasive species distribution models. Number of species is the number of invasive species whose predicted distribution overlap within the area.

Number of Species	Area Predicted (hectares)	Area Predicted / Area of Park (%)
0	11,430.7	41.0
1	6,142.2	22.0
2	4,565.4	16.4
3	1,362.8	4.9
4	1,695.8	6.1
5	1,439.9	5.2
6	708.3	2.5
7	377.7	1.4
8	183.2	0.7
9	3.0	0.0

[1.2%] of total hemlock community area). Figure 21 depicts *T. canadensis* communities stands ranked according to susceptibility to invasion.

Levels of infestation were assessed at a total of 1,204 assessment points representing 1,199 plant community polygons. A large percentage of accuracy assessment points contained either no invasive species (33.6%) or only one species (16.9%). In general; successional, riparian, and mesic terrestrial communities had the greatest invasive species abundance and frequency per sampling point (Table 9). Cliff complexes and dry terrestrial communities had lower invasive species abundance and frequency per sampling point. Figure 22 depicts the distribution of communities with high and low invasive species activity.

Rare communities with a high mean invasive index included Calcareous Fens, Shale Scree Slopes, Marl Fens, and Calcareous Riverside Outcrops (Table 10). The invasive species that showed high abundance or frequency in these rare communities are listed below:

Rocky Woodland / Cliff / Scree complexes: *Ailanthus altissima* and *Microstegium vimineum* are particularly abundant. These associations can also contain: *Alliaria petiolata, Berberis thunbergii, Celastrus orbiculatus, Centaurea biebersteinii, Elaeagnus umbellata, Euonymus alatus, Coronilla varia, Lonicera morrowii, Rosa multiflora, Rubus phoenicolasius,* and *Verbascum thapsus*

Marl Fen: *Berberis thunbergii, Celastrus orbiculatus, Lythrum salicaria,* and *Rosa multiflora* can be abundant.

Calcareous Fen: *Lythrum salicaria* can be abundant. This association can also contain *Berberis thunbergii, Elaeagnus umbellata, Euonymus alatus, Lonicera morrowii,* and *Rosa multiflora*.

Calcareous Riverside Outcrop / Calcareous Riverside Seep: *Lythrum salicaria, Tussilago farara,* and *Polygonum cuspidatum* can be abundant.

Big Bluestem - Indian Grass River Grassland: No invasives were abundant, however, *Elaeagnus umbellata, Lonicera morrowii, Polygonum cuspidatum, Lythrum salicaria,* and *Alliaria petiolata* can be present.

Pitch Pine - Mixed Hardwood Rocky Summit: *Ailanthus altissima, Alliaria petiolata, Centaurea biebersteinii,* and *Verbascum thapsus* can be common.

No invasive species were observed in this study in the following rare communities: Boulder Vernal Pool Sparse Vegetation, Eastern Woodland Vernal Pool Sparse Vegetation, Red Maple - Black Spruce - Highbush Blueberry Palustrine Woodland, Highbush Blueberry - Leatherleaf Wetland, Leatherleaf Peatland, and Acidic Seep.

Table 10. Mean infestation score and number of polygons for rare communities containing sampling points.

Community Type	Number of Polygons	Mean Infestation Score
Calcareous Riverside Outcrop / Calcareous Riverside Seep	2	2.8
Marl Fen	1	2.5
Shale Scree Slope	12	2.3
Calcareous Fen	3	1.8
Hickory - Eastern Red-cedar Rocky Woodland / Shale Scree Slope	1	1.5
Big Bluestem - Indiangrass Riverine Grassland	3	1.0
Hickory - Eastern Red-cedar Rocky Woodland / Sparsely Veg. Cliff	22	0.8
Hickory - Eastern Red-cedar Rocky Woodland	20	0.6
Sparsely Vegetated Cliff	7	0.3
Pitch Pine - Mixed Hardwood Rocky Summit	25	0.1
Pitch Pine - Mixed Hard. Rocky Summit / Eastern Red-cedar Forest	1	0.0

Table 9. Total and average abundance, frequency, and number of invasive species observed in vegetation associations in the Delaware Water Gap National Recreation Area. Total abundance is the sum of all species' cover classes and total frequency is the sum of all species occurrences.

Association	Number of Sample Points	Number of Invasive Species Observed	Number of Invasive Species Observed / Number Points Sampled	Total Abundance	Total Abundance / Number Points Sampled	Total Frequency	Total Frequency / Number Points Sampled	Mean Infestation Score
SUCCESSIONAL	267			24,417	91.45	850	3.18	2.17
Built-up Land	1	1	1.00	10	10.00	1	1.00	1.00
Conifer Plantation	39	16	0.41	1,928	49.44	99	2.54	1.71
Eastern Red-cedar Forest	7	8	1.14	792	113.14	26	3.71	2.79
Eastern Red-cedar Forest / Old Field	4	7	1.75	351	87.75	11	2.75	2.00
Eastern White Pine - Successional Hardwood Forest	35	13	0.37	1,735	49.57	77	2.20	1.42
Highbush Blueberry - Steeplebush Wetland / Successional Shrubland	1	3	3.00	80	80.00	3	3.00	3.00
Japanese Knotweed Herbaceous Vegetation / Successional Shrubland	1	6	6.00	101	101.00	6	6.00	3.50
Northeastern Modified Successional Forest	76	23	0.30	10,874	143.08	329	4.33	2.81
Old Field	33	19	0.58	1,789	54.21	77	2.33	1.61
Old Field / Built-up Land	1	2	2.00	120	120.00	2	2.00	2.50
Pitch Pine - Mixed Hardwood Rocky Summit / Eastern Red-cedar Forest	1	0	0.00	0	0.00	0	0.00	0.00
Reed Canarygrass Riverine Grassland / Northeastern Modified Successional Forest	1	2	2.00	70	70.00	2	2.00	2.00
Successional Bear Oak - Heath Shrubland / Northeastern Modified Successional Forest	1	0	0.00	0	0.00	0	0.00	0.00
Successional Eastern White Pine Woodland	18	16	0.89	1,456	80.89	61	3.39	2.11
Successional Eastern White Pine Woodland / Eastern Red-cedar Forest	1	1	1.00	10	10.00	1	1.00	1.00
Successional Shrubland	42	24	0.57	4,651	110.74	135	3.21	2.44
Wooded Successional Old Field	5	12	2.40	450	90.00	20	4.00	2.50
RIPARIAN	155			12,938	83.47	456	2.94	2.32
Big Bluestem - Indiangrass Riverine Grassland	3	4	1.33	31	10.33	4	1.33	0.00
Big Bluestem - Indiangrass Riverine Grassland / Sycamore - Mixed Hardwood Riverine Shrubland	1	1	1.00	10	10.00	1	1.00	0.00
Bitternut Hickory Lowland Forest	7	10	1.43	890	127.14	29	4.14	2.70
Calcareous Riverside Outcrop / Calcareous Riverside Seep	3	7	2.33	440	146.67	9	3.00	2.75
Japanese Knotweed Herbaceous Vegetation	4	5	1.25	254	63.50	9	2.25	2.13
Reed Canarygrass Riverine Grassland	4	7	1.75	122	30.50	9	2.25	1.63
River	7	6	0.86	342	48.86	11	1.57	0.00
Riverine Scour Vegetation	15	13	0.87	830	55.33	37	2.47	1.85
Riverine Scour Vegetation / Sycamore - Mixed Hardwood Riverine Shrubland	1	1	1.00	10	10.00	1	1.00	1.00
Silver Maple Floodplain Forest	28	8	0.29	2,068	73.86	69	2.46	2.16
Sugar Maple Floodplain Forest	18	12	0.67	1,353	75.17	58	3.22	2.50
Sugar Maple Floodplain Forest / Bitternut Hickory Floodplain Forest	2	7	3.50	113	56.50	9	4.50	2.50
Sycamore - Mixed Hardwood Floodplain Forest	31	19	0.61	3,921	126.48	132	4.26	2.76
Sycamore - Mixed Hardwood Riverine Shrubland	17	8	0.47	1,037	61.00	35	2.06	2.04
Sycamore (Willow) - Mixed Hardwood Riverine Dwarf Shrubland	3	5	1.67	103	34.33	8	2.67	1.67
Sycamore Floodplain Forest	11	8	0.73	1,414	128.55	35	3.18	2.65

Table 9. Total and average abundance, frequency, and number of invasive species observed in vegetation associations in the Delaware Water Gap National Recreation Area (continued). Total abundance is the sum of all species' cover classes and total frequency is the sum of all species occurrences.

Association	Number of Sample Points	Number of Invasive Species Observed	Number of Invasive Species Observed / Number Points Sampled	Total Abundance	Total Abundance / Number Points Sampled	Total Frequency	Total Frequency / Number Points Sampled	Mean Infestation Score
MESIC TERRESTRIAL	**209**	10	1.00	**13,731**	**65.70**	**569**	**2.72**	**1.87**
Black Walnut Bottomland Forest	10	10	1.00	1,101	110.10	36	3.60	2.80
Eastern Hemlock - Northern Hardwood Forest	24	12	0.50	802	33.42	41	1.71	1.20
Eastern Hemlock - Northern Hardwood Forest / Northern Red Oak - Mixed Hardwood Forest	1	3	3.00	21	21.00	3	3.00	1.50
Northern Red Oak - Mixed Hardwood Forest	57	18	0.32	3,410	59.82	148	2.60	1.75
Red Maple - Sweet Birch Hardwood Forest	38	11	0.29	2,595	68.29	103	2.71	1.93
Sugar Maple - American Basswood Forest	8	9	1.13	756	94.50	31	3.88	2.80
Sugar Maple - American Beech - Sweet Birch Forest	51	14	0.27	3,662	71.80	150	2.94	1.96
Sugar Maple - American Beech - Sweet Birch Forest / Northern Red Oak - Mixed Hardwood Forest	3	2	0.67	131	43.67	4	1.33	1.50
Tuliptree - Beech - Maple Forest	17	12	0.71	1,253	73.71	53	3.12	2.17
PALUSTRINE	**204**			**10,400**	**50.98**	**380**	**1.86**	**1.50**
Acidic Seep	1	0	0.00	0	0.00	0	0.00	0.00
Alder Wetland	4	2	0.50	80	20.00	3	0.75	1.25
Bottomland Mixed Hardwood Palustrine Forest	17	11	0.65	1,624	95.53	51	3.00	2.23
Bottomland Oak Palustrine Forest	10	8	0.80	771	77.10	28	2.80	2.25
Buttonbush Wetland	5	5	1.00	210	42.00	6	1.20	1.00
Calcareous Fen	5	6	1.20	281	56.20	14	2.80	1.83
Cattail Marsh	1	1	1.00	1	1.00	1	1.00	1.00
Eastern Hemlock - Mixed Hardwood Palustrine Forest	7	1	0.14	70	10.00	2	0.29	0.50
Eastern Woodland Vernal Pool Sparse Vegetation	1	0	0.00	0	0.00	0	0.00	0.00
Hairyfruit Sedge Wetland	3	7	2.33	81	27.00	9	3.00	1.67
Highbush Blueberry - Leatherleaf Wetland	3	0	0.00	0	0.00	0	0.00	0.00
Highbush Blueberry - Steeplebush Wetland	13	6	0.46	543	41.77	17	1.31	1.29
Marl Seep Fen	2	4	2.00	250	125.00	5	2.50	0.00
Mixed Forb Marsh	11	10	0.91	484	44.00	17	1.55	1.50
Pond	4	1	0.25	10	2.50	1	0.25	0.25
Red Maple - Black Spruce - Highbush Blueberry Palustrine Woodland / Eastern Hemlock - Mixed Hardwood Palustrine Forest	1	0	0.00	0	0.00	0	0.00	0.00
Red Maple - Highbush Blueberry Palustrine Forest	20	5	0.25	184	9.20	12	0.60	0.43
Red Maple Palustrine Forest	26	10	0.38	1,286	49.46	58	2.23	1.82
Silky Dogwood Successional Palustrine Shrubland	26	11	0.42	2,606	100.23	81	3.12	2.40
Silky Dogwood Successional Palustrine Shrubland / Alder Wetland	1	3	3.00	30	30.00	3	3.00	2.00
Silky Dogwood Successional Palustrine Shrubland / Tussock Sedge Marsh	1	1	1.00	60	60.00	1	1.00	2.00
Silky Dogwood Successional Palustrine Shrubland / Wet Meadow	1	8	8.00	271	271.00	8	8.00	3.50
Successional Bear Oak - Heath Shrubland / Highbush Blueberry - Steeplebush Wetland	1	0	0.00	0	0.00	0	0.00	0.00
Tussock Sedge Marsh	10	5	0.50	331	33.10	14	1.40	1.40
Wet Meadow	30	10	0.33	1,227	40.90	49	1.63	1.35

Table 9. Total and average abundance, frequency, and number of invasive species observed in vegetation associations in the Delaware Water Gap National Recreation Area (continued). Total abundance is the sum of all species' cover classes and total frequency is the sum of all species occurrences.

Association	Number of Sample Points	Number of Invasive Species Observed	Number of Invasive Species Observed / Number Points Sampled	Total Abundance	Total Abundance / Number Points Sampled	Total Frequency	Total Frequency / Number Points Sampled	Mean Infestation Score
CLIFF COMPLEXES	**86**			**1,715**	**19.94**	**99**	**1.15**	**0.82**
Hickory - Eastern Red-cedar Rocky Woodland	21	7	0.33	215	10.24	16	0.76	0.58
Hickory - Eastern Red-cedar Rocky Woodland / Shale Scree Slope	1	5	5.00	23	23.00	5	5.00	1.50
Hickory - Eastern Red-cedar Rocky Woodland / Sparsely Vegetated Cliff	27	11	0.41	340	12.59	28	1.04	0.75
Dry Hickory Ridgetop Forest / Hickory - Eastern Red-cedar Rocky Woodland	1	3	3.00	21	21.00	3	3.00	1.50
Little Bluestem Grassland / Sparsely Vegetated Cliff	1	1	1.00	1	1.00	1	1.00	1.00
Oak - Birch Talus Forest / Sandstone Talus	4	2	0.50	20	5.00	2	0.50	0.33
Sandstone Talus	10	1	0.10	10	1.00	1	0.10	0.10
Shale Scree Slope	13	12	0.92	1,064	81.85	40	3.08	2.25
DRY TERRESTRIAL (includes high ridgetop wetlands)	**433**		**0.92**	**3,930**	**9.08**	**275**	**0.64**	**0.50**
Bear Oak - Wavy Hairgrass Shrubland	9	7	0.78	102	11.33	7	0.78	0.56
Bear Oak - Wavy Hairgrass Shrubland / Dry Oak - Heath Forest	1	0	0.00	0	0.00	0	0.00	0.00
Boulder Vernal Pool Sparse Vegetation	4	0	0.00	0	0.00	0	0.00	0.00
Dry Eastern Hemlock - Oak Forest	52	9	0.17	340	6.54	28	0.54	0.47
Dry Eastern White Pine - Oak Forest	36	11	0.31	326	9.06	28	0.78	0.47
Dry Hickory Ridgetop Forest	26	6	0.23	227	8.73	14	0.54	0.50
Dry Oak - Heath Forest	85	11	0.13	216	2.54	17	0.20	0.22
Dry Oak - Heath Forest / Oak - Birch Talus Forest	4	0	0.00	0	0.00	0	0.00	0.00
Dry Oak - Mixed Hardwood Forest	74	11	0.15	1,146	15.49	74	1.00	0.73
Eastern Hemlock Forest	22	7	0.32	286	13.00	19	0.86	0.97
Eastern White Pine Forest	27	11	0.41	526	19.48	37	1.37	1.04
Leatherleaf Peatland	2	0	0.00	0	0.00	0	0.00	0.00
Little Bluestem Grassland	5	4	0.80	71	14.20	8	1.60	1.00
Oak - Birch Talus Forest	28	12	0.43	514	18.36	30	1.07	0.68
Pitch Pine - Mixed Hardwood Rocky Summit	27	4	0.15	32	1.19	5	0.19	0.12
Red Maple - Black Spruce - Highbush Blueberry Palustrine Woodland	2	0	0.00	0	0.00	0	0.00	0.00
Successional Bear Oak - Heath Shrubland	20	3	0.15	81	4.05	4	0.20	0.28
Successional Bear Oak - Heath Shrubland / Dry Eastern White Pine - Oak Forest	1	0	0.00	0	0.00	0	0.00	0.00
Successional Bear Oak - Heath Shrubland / Dry Oak - Heath Forest	1	0	0.00	0	0.00	0	0.00	0.00
Wavy Hairgrass - Common Sheep Sorrell Rock Outcrop	6	3	0.50	63	10.50	4	0.67	0.67
Wavy Hairgrass - Common Sheep Sorrell Rock Outcrop / Dry Oak - Heath Forest	1	0	0.00	0	0.00	0	0.00	0.00

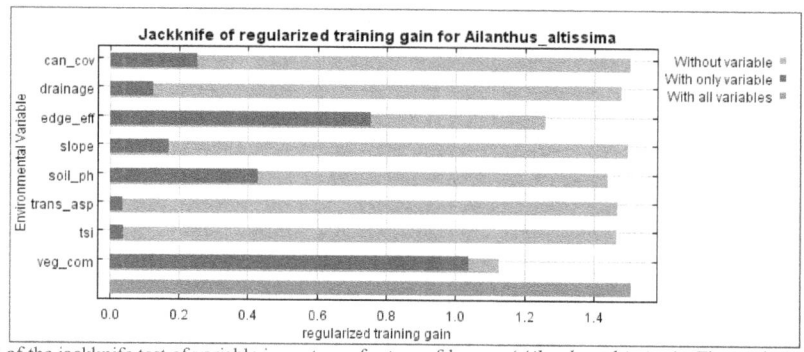

Figure 1. Results of the jackknife test of variable importance for tree-of-heaven (*Ailanthus altissima*). The environmental variable with highest gain when used in isolation is vegetation community (veg_com), which therefore appears to have the most useful information by itself. The environmental variable that decreases the gain the most when it is omitted is vegetation community (veg_com), which therefore appears to have the most information that isn't present in the other variables

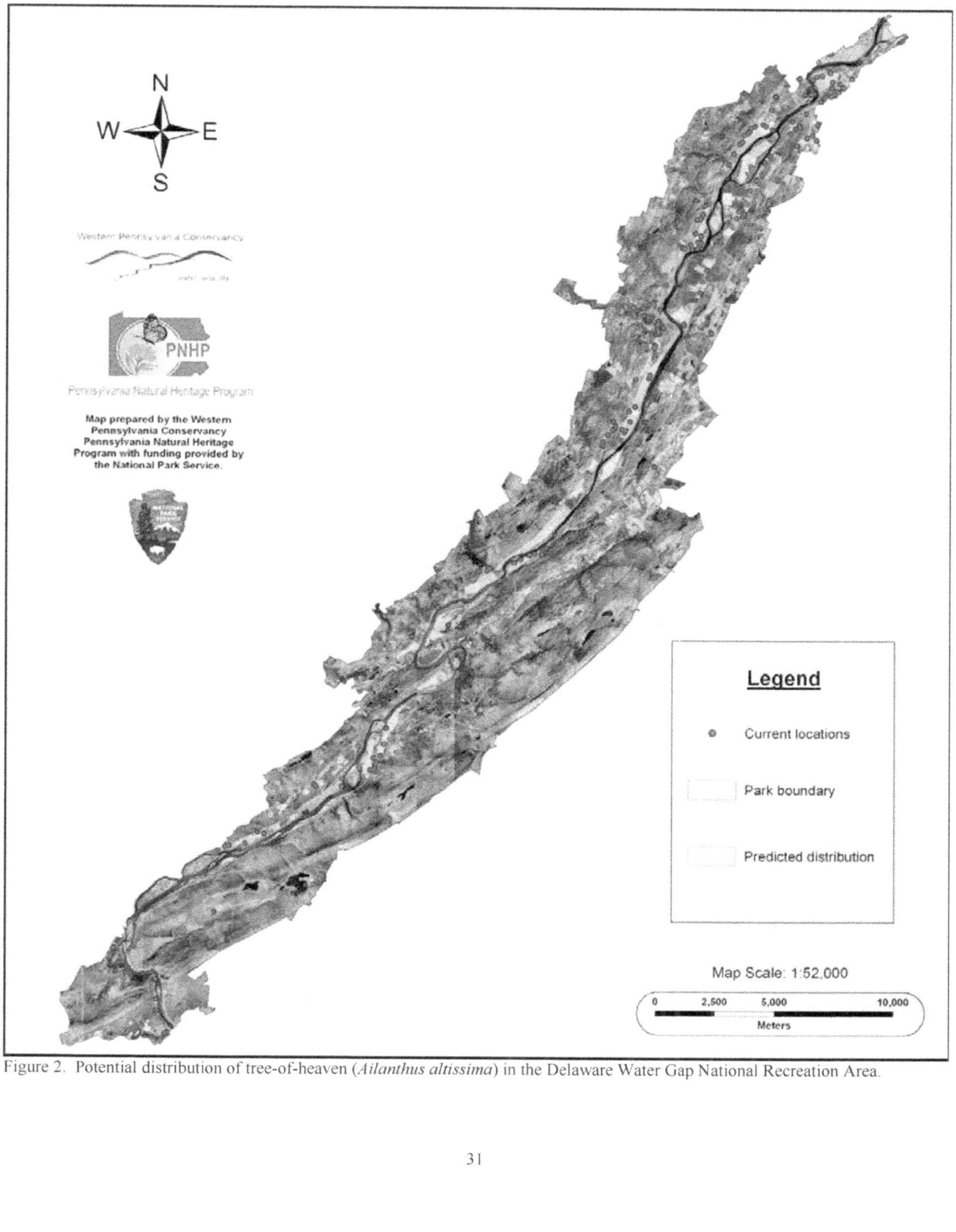

Figure 2. Potential distribution of tree-of-heaven (*Ailanthus altissima*) in the Delaware Water Gap National Recreation Area.

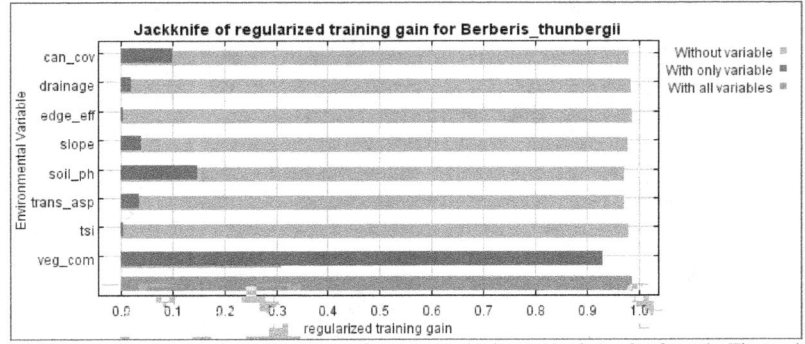

Figure 3. Results of the jackknife test of variable importance for Japanese barberry (*Berberis thunbergii*). The environmental variable with highest gain when used in isolation is vegetation community (veg_com), which therefore appears to have the most useful information by itself. The environmental variable that decreases the gain the most when it is omitted is vegetation community (veg_com), which therefore appears to have the most information that isn't present in the other variables.

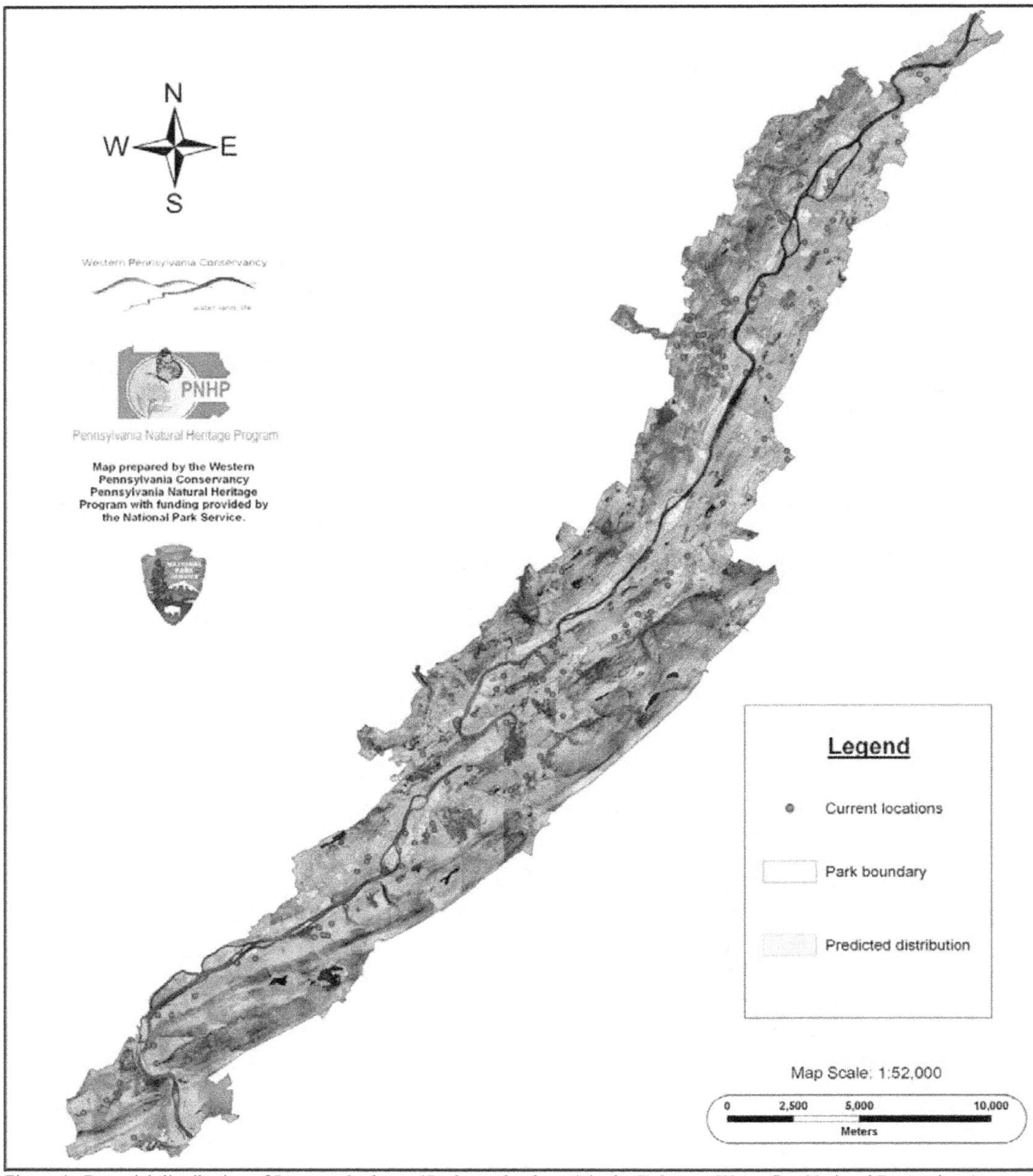

Figure 4. Potential distribution of Japanese barberry (*Berberis thunbergii*) in the Delaware Water Gap National Recreation Area.

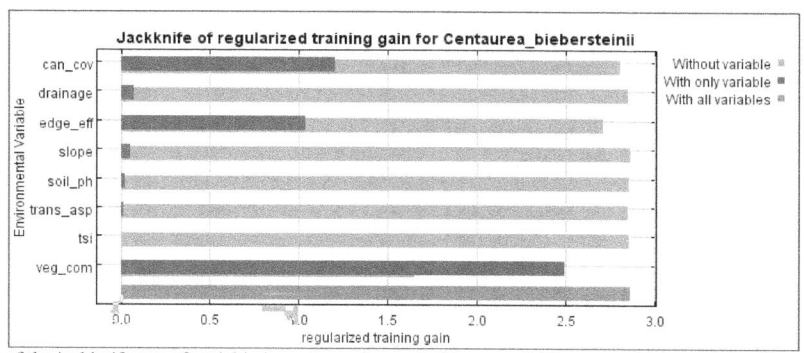

Figure 5. Results of the jackknife test of variable importance for spotted knapweed (*Centaurea biebersteinii*). The environmental variable with highest gain when used in isolation is vegetation community (veg_com), which therefore appears to have the most useful information by itself. The environmental variable that decreases the gain the most when it is omitted is vegetation community (veg_com), which therefore appears to have the most information that isn't present in the other variables.

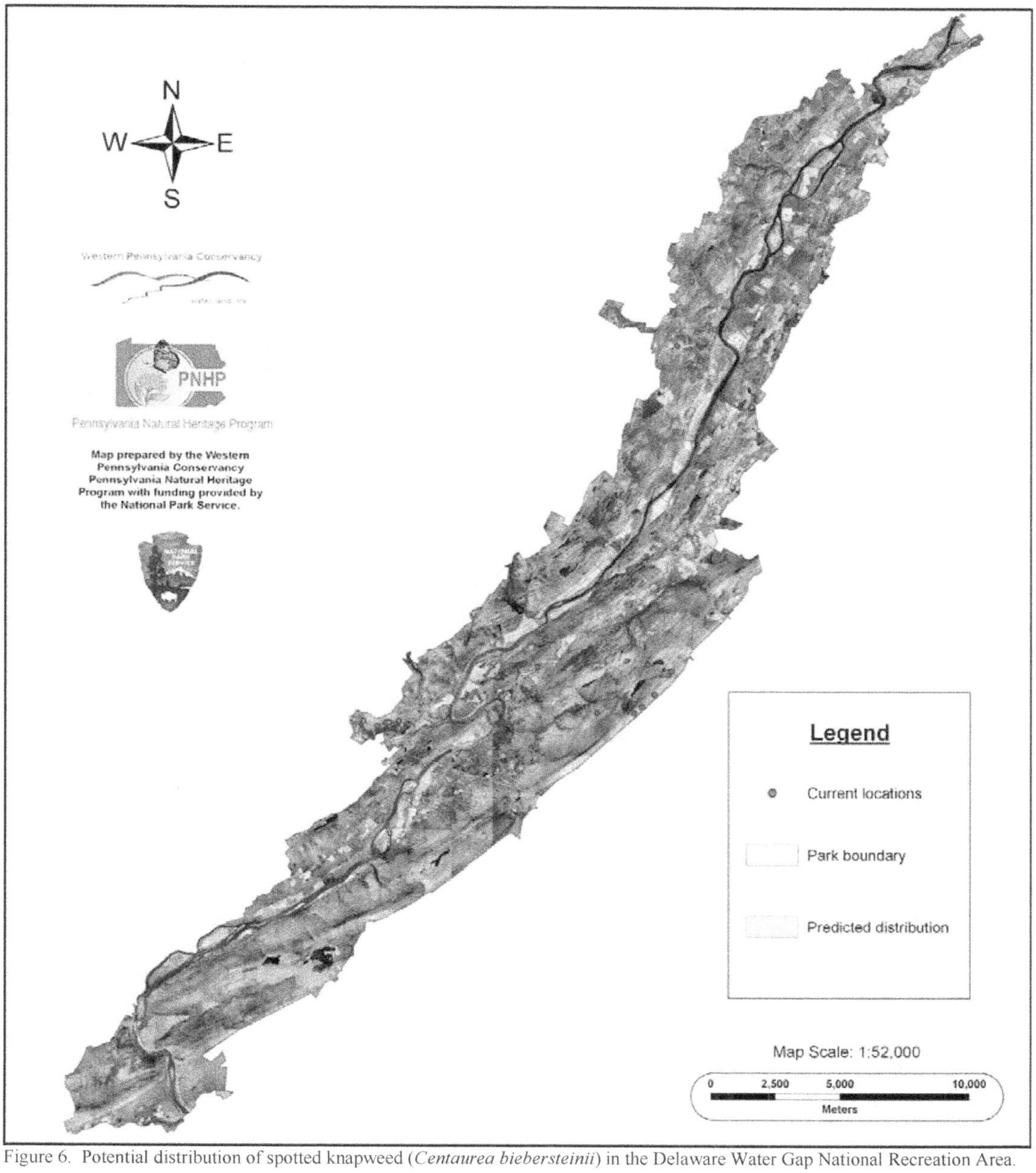

Figure 6. Potential distribution of spotted knapweed (*Centaurea biebersteinii*) in the Delaware Water Gap National Recreation Area.

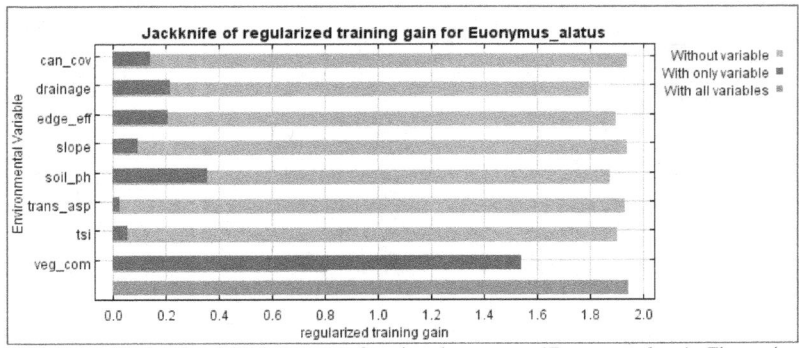

Figure 7. Results of the jackknife test of variable importance for winged euonymus (*Euonymus alatus*). The environmental variable with highest gain when used in isolation is vegetation community (veg_com), which therefore appears to have the most useful information by itself. The environmental variable that decreases the gain the most when it is omitted is vegetation community (veg_com), which therefore appears to have the most information that isn't present in the other variables.

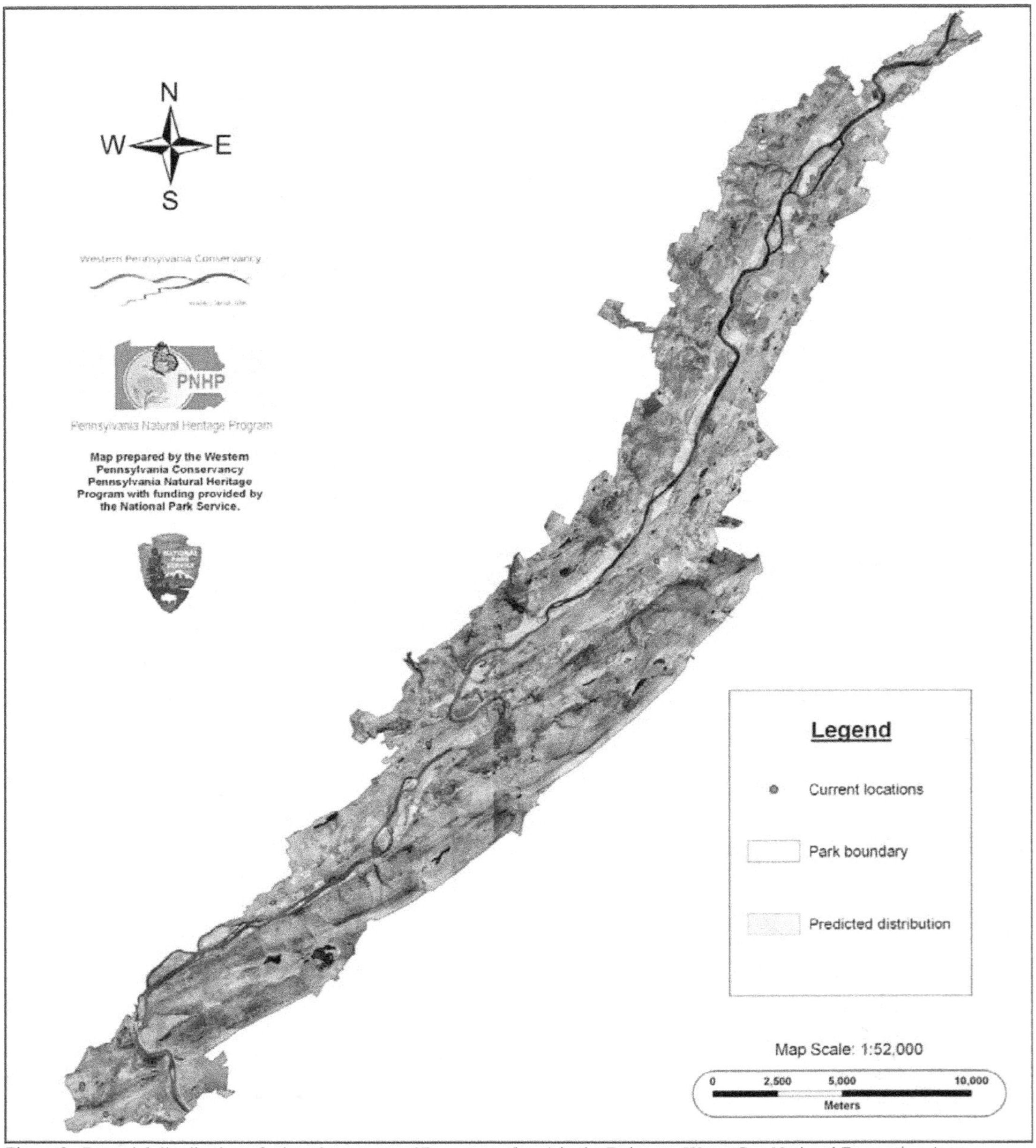

Figure 8. Potential distribution of winged euonymus (*Euonymus alatus*) in the Delaware Water Gap National Recreation Area.

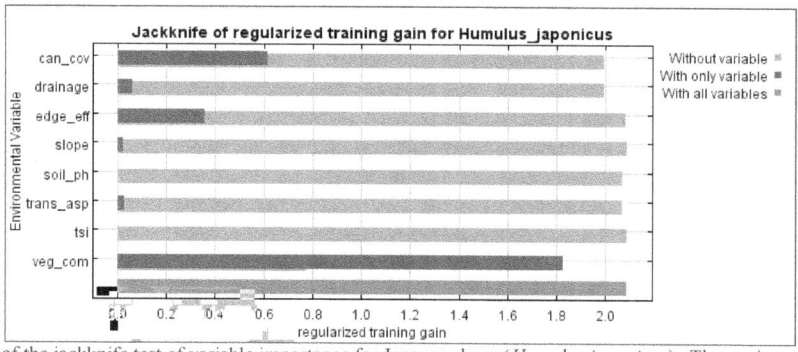

Figure 9. Results of the jackknife test of variable importance for Japanese hops (*Humulus japonicus*). The environmental variable with highest gain when used in isolation is vegetation community (veg_com), which therefore appears to have the most useful information by itself. The environmental variable that decreases the gain the most when it is omitted is vegetation community (veg_com), which therefore appears to have the most information that isn't present in the other variables.

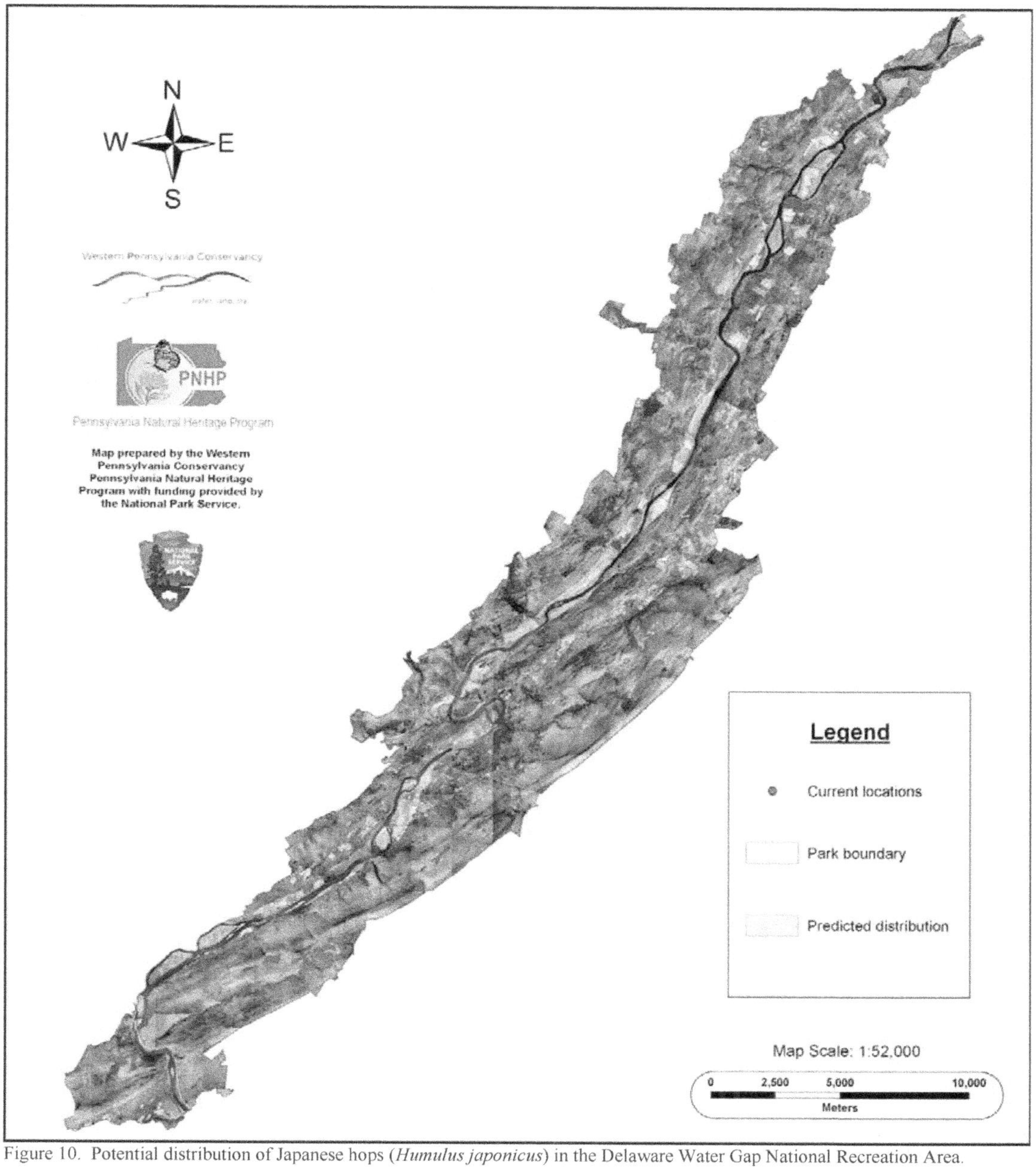

Figure 10. Potential distribution of Japanese hops (*Humulus japonicus*) in the Delaware Water Gap National Recreation Area.

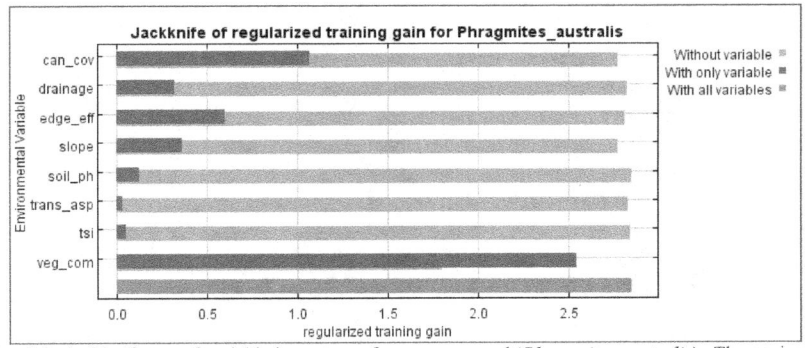

Figure 11. Results of the jackknife test of variable importance for common reed (*Phragmites australis*). The environmental variable with highest gain when used in isolation is vegetation community (veg_com), which therefore appears to have the most useful information by itself. The environmental variable that decreases the gain the most when it is omitted is vegetation community (veg_com), which therefore appears to have the most information that isn't present in the other variables.

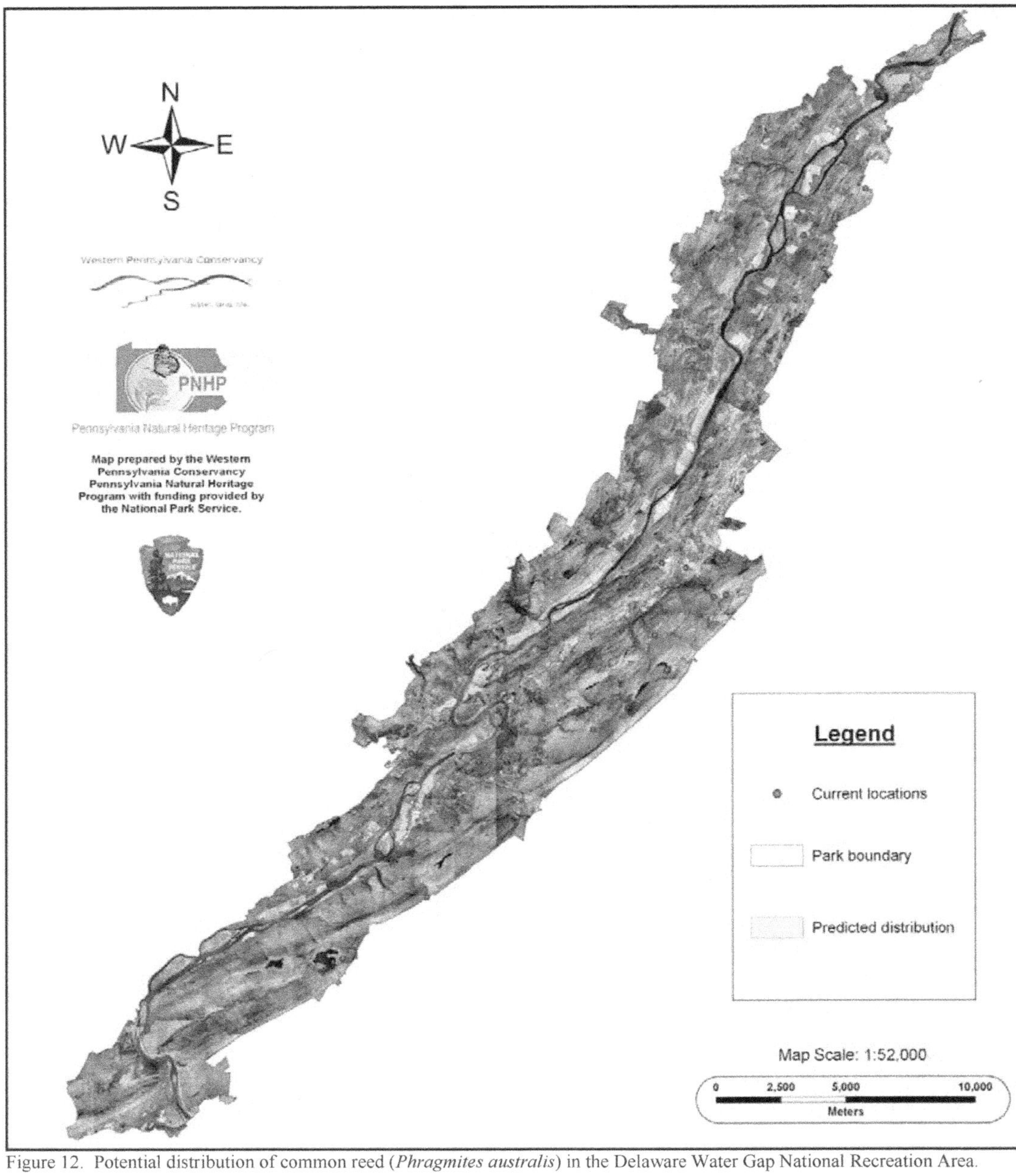

Figure 12. Potential distribution of common reed (*Phragmites australis*) in the Delaware Water Gap National Recreation Area.

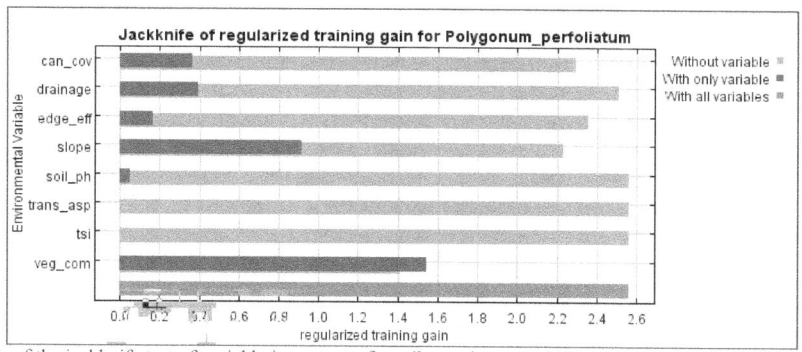

Figure 13. Results of the jackknife test of variable importance for mile-a-minute (*Polygonum perfoliatum*). The environmental variable with highest gain when used in isolation is vegetation community (veg_com), which therefore appears to have the most useful information by itself. The environmental variable that decreases the gain the most when it is omitted is vegetation community (veg_com), which therefore appears to have the most information that isn't present in the other variables.

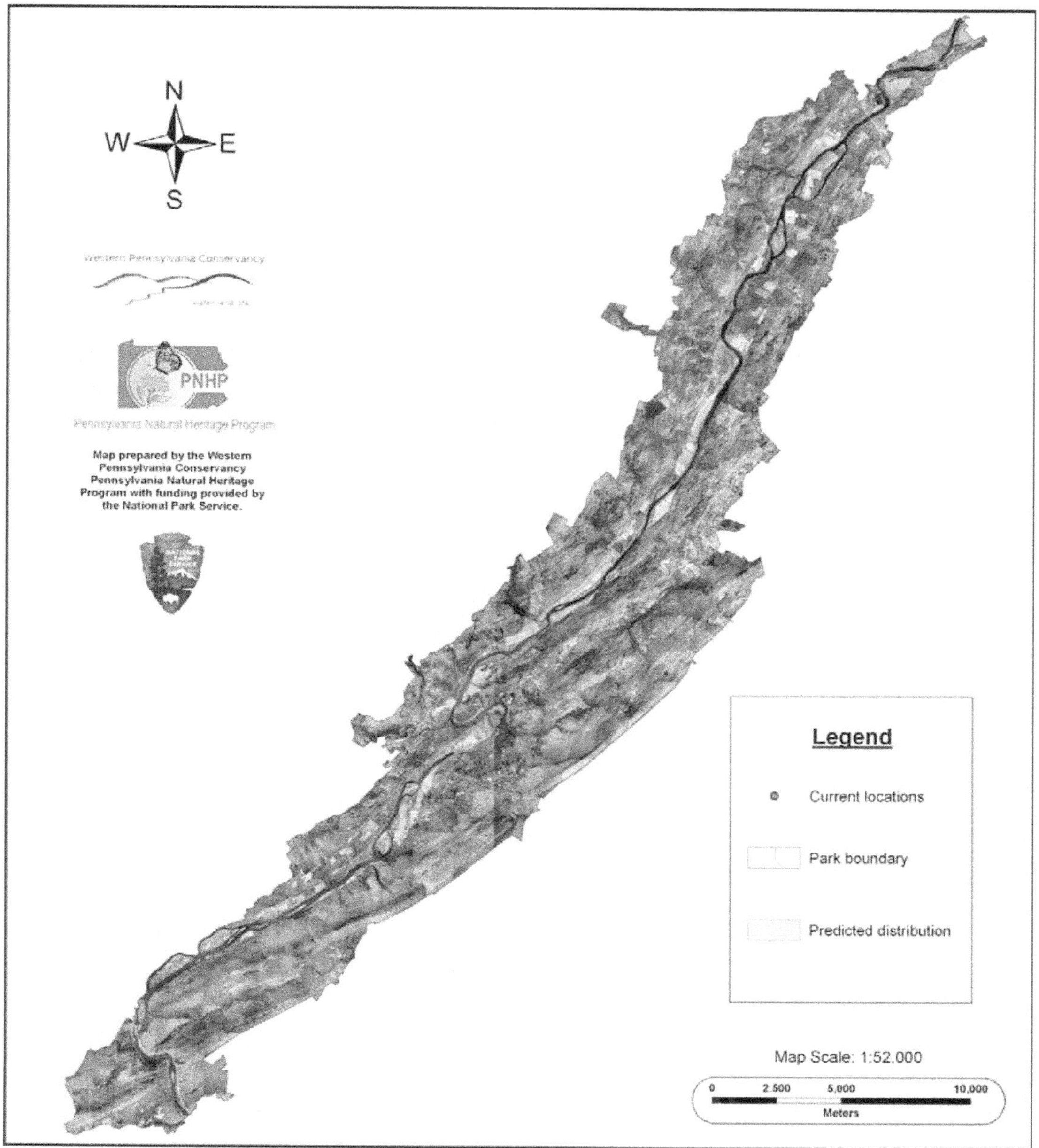

Figure 14. Potential distribution of mile-a-minute weed (*Polygonum perfoliatum*) in the Delaware Water Gap National Recreation Area.

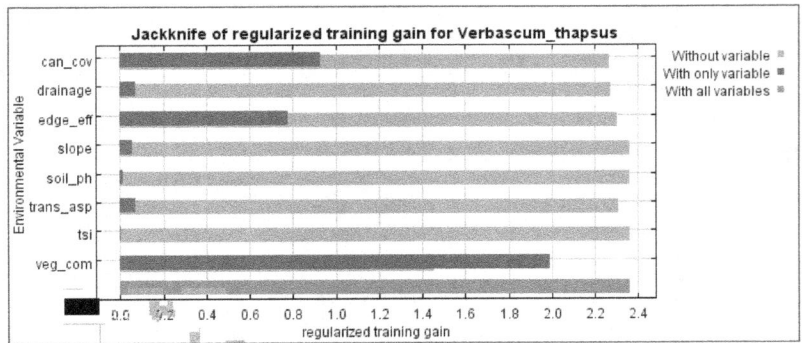

Figure 15. Results of the jackknife test of variable importance for common mullein (*Verbascum thapsus*). The environmental variable with highest gain when used in isolation is vegetation community (veg_com), which therefore appears to have the most useful information by itself. The environmental variable that decreases the gain the most when it is omitted is vegetation community (veg_com), which therefore appears to have the most information that isn't present in the other variables.

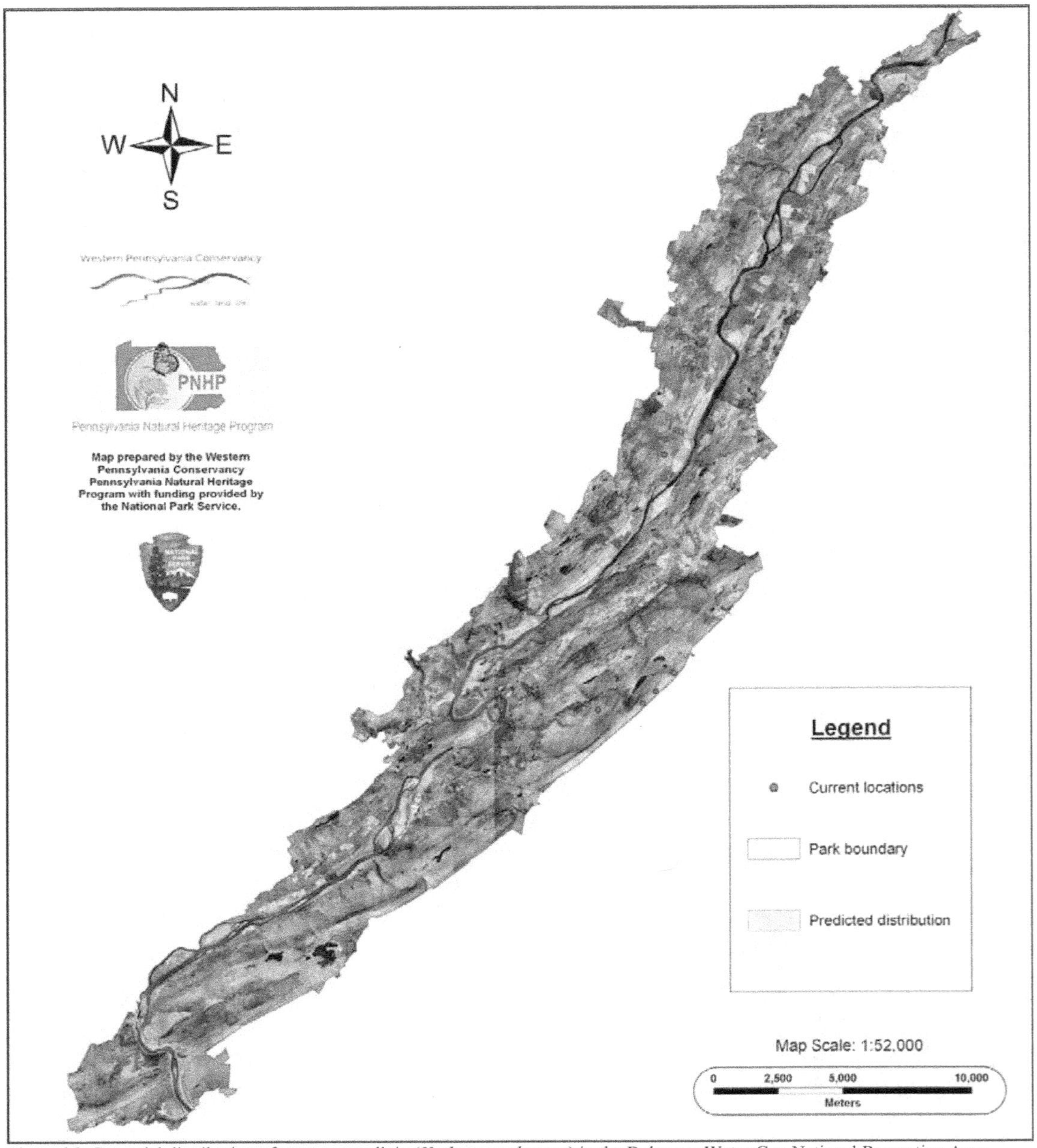

Figure 16. Potential distribution of common mullein (*Verbascum thapsus*) in the Delaware Water Gap National Recreation Area.

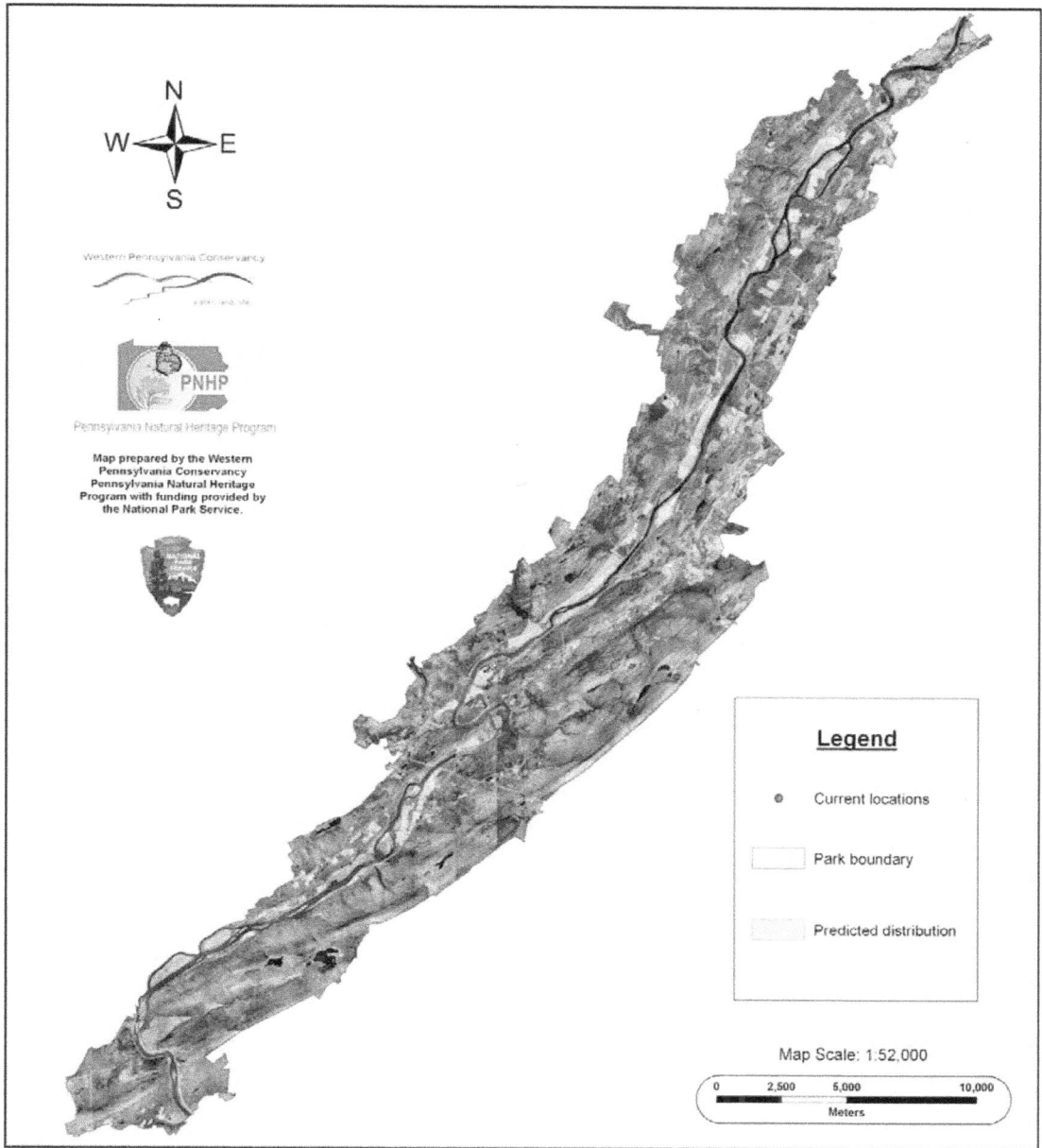

Figure 17. Potential distribution of Norway maple (*Acer platanoides*) in the Delaware Water Gap National Recreation Area.

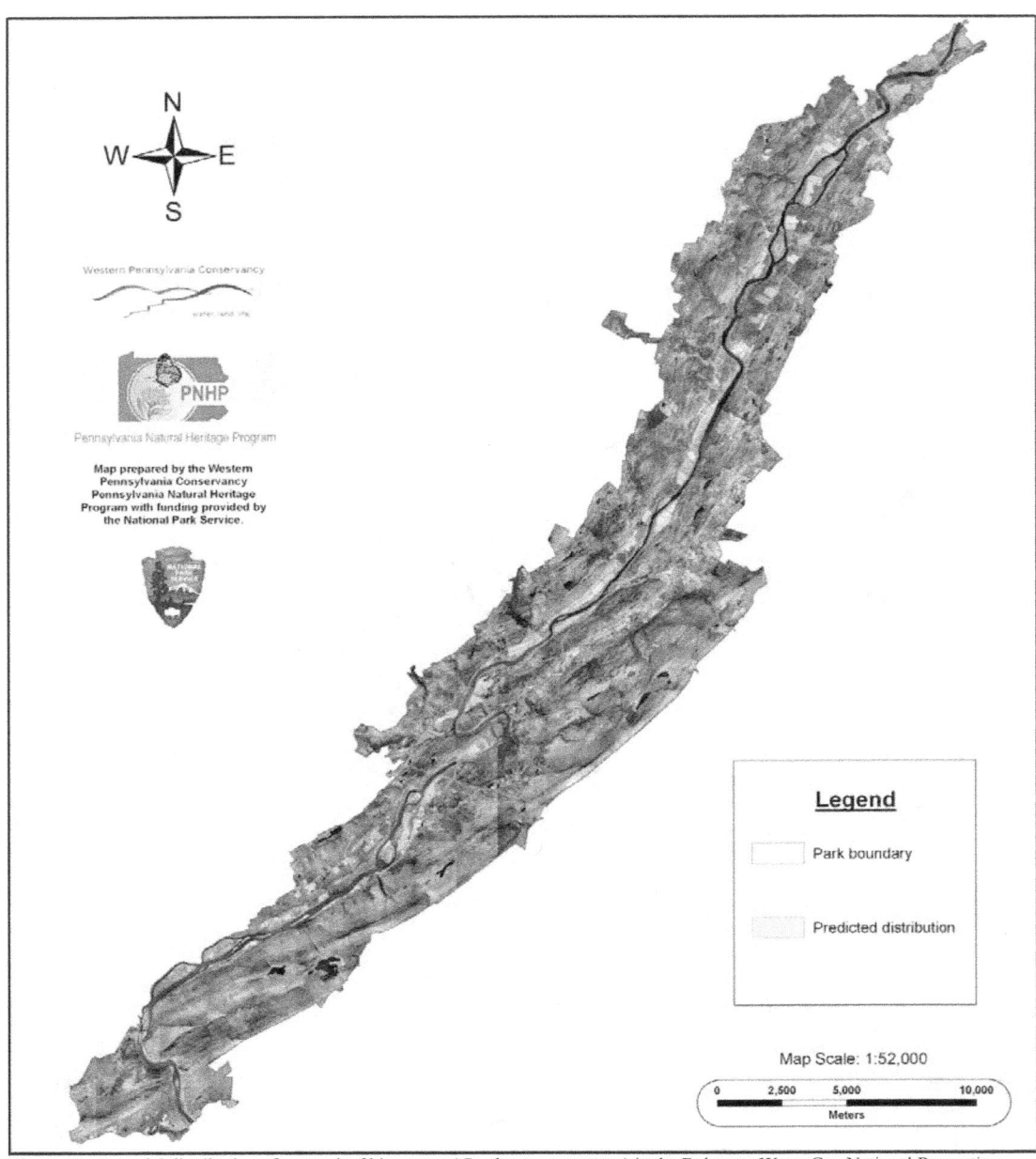

Figure 18. Potential distribution of narrowleaf bittercress (*Cardamine impatiens*) in the Delaware Water Gap National Recreation Area.

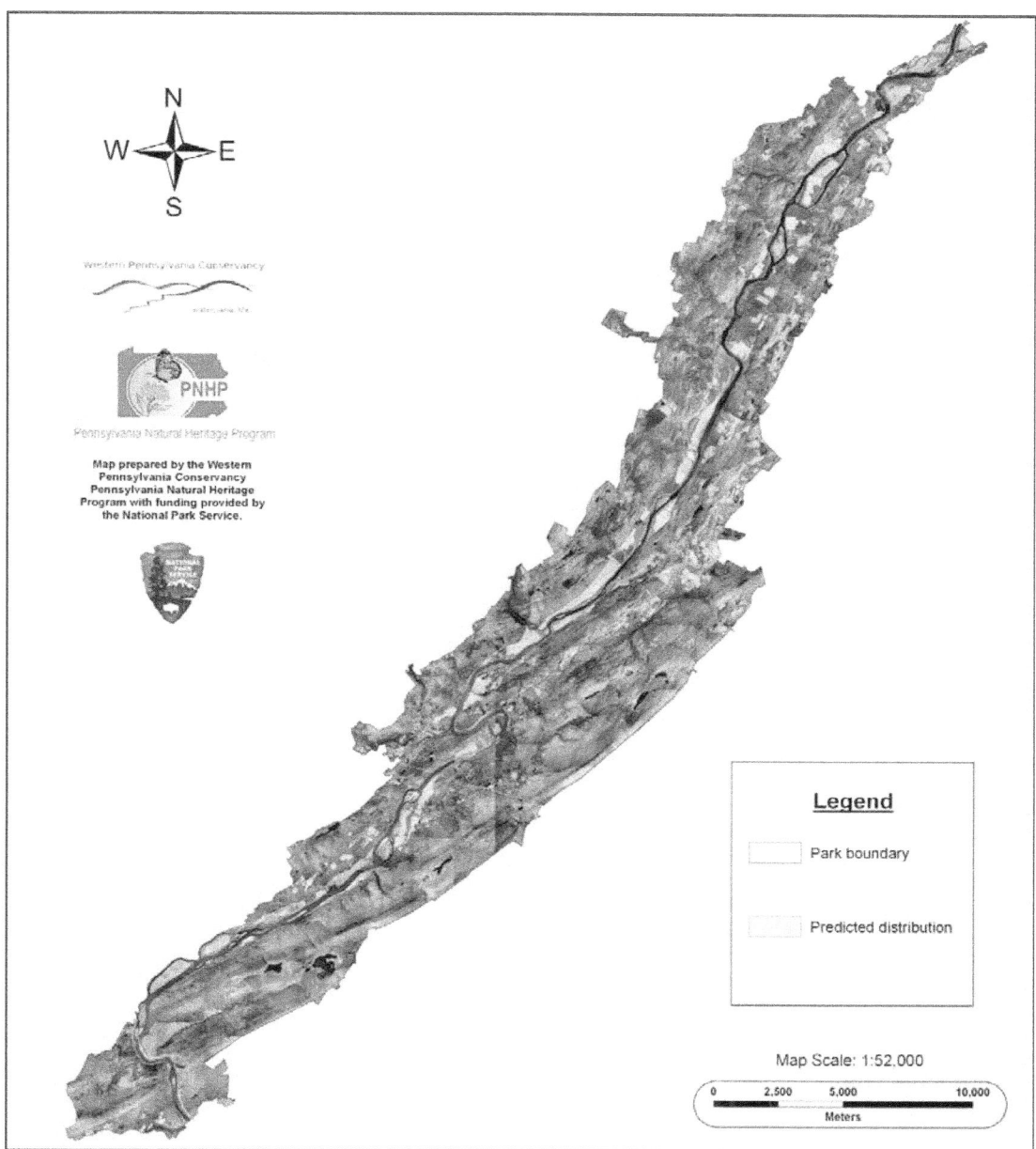

Figure 19. Potential distribution of fig buttercup (*Ranunculus ficaria*) in the Delaware Water Gap National Recreation Area.

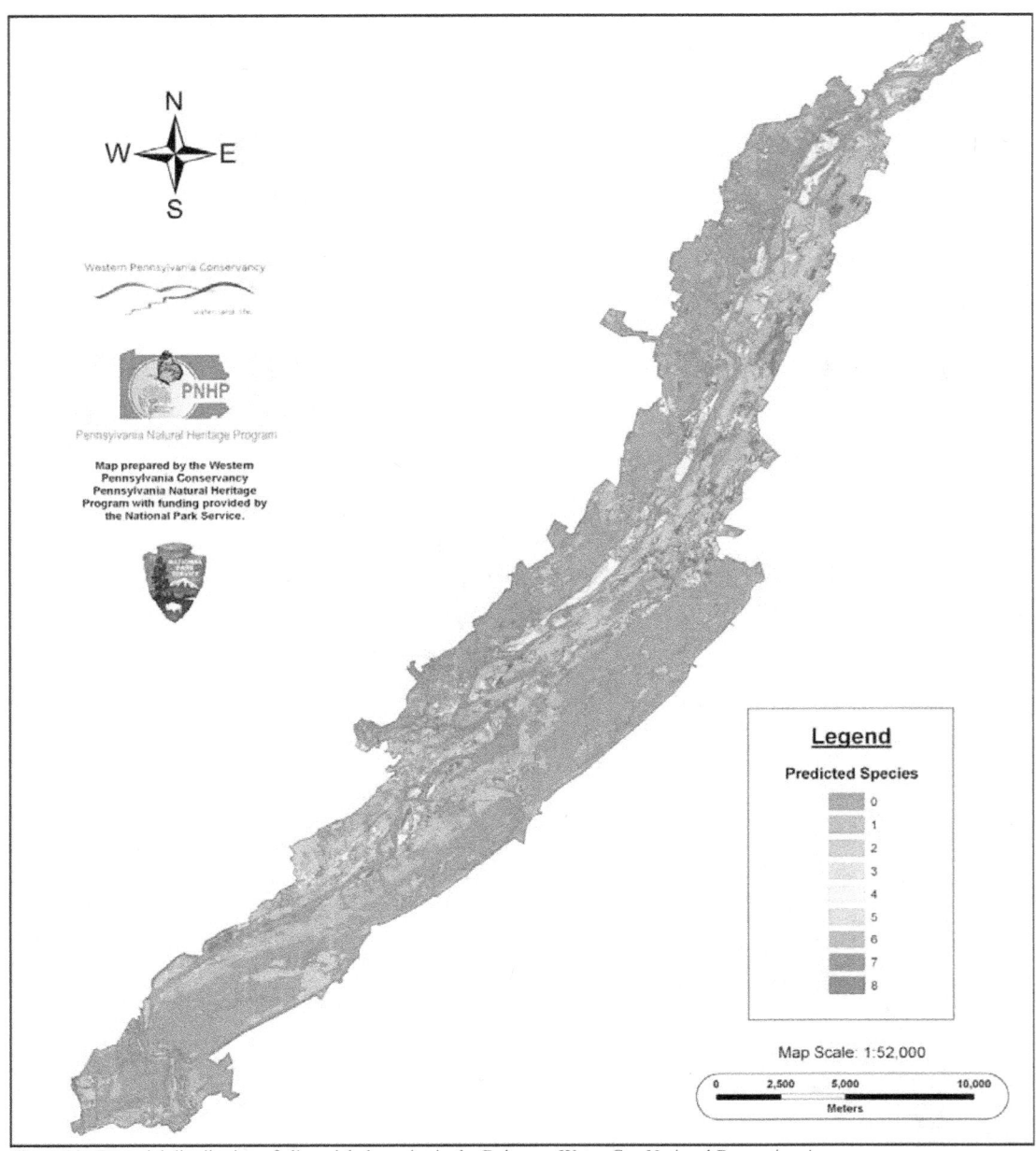

Figure 20. Potential distribution of all modeled species in the Delaware Water Gap National Recreation Area.

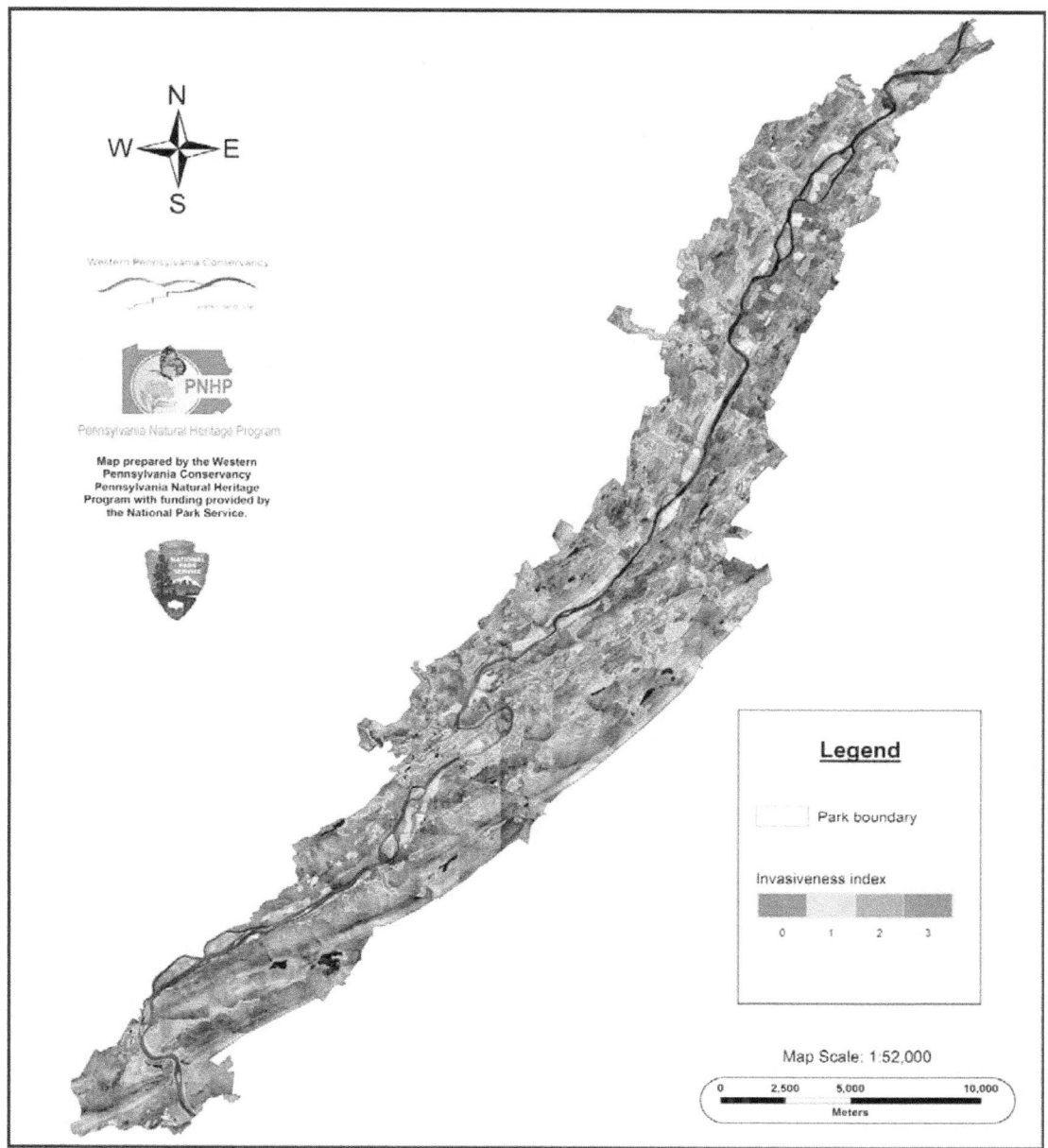

Figure 21. Susceptibility of eastern hemlock (*Tsuga canadensis*) communities to invasion in the Delaware Water Gap National Recreation Area.

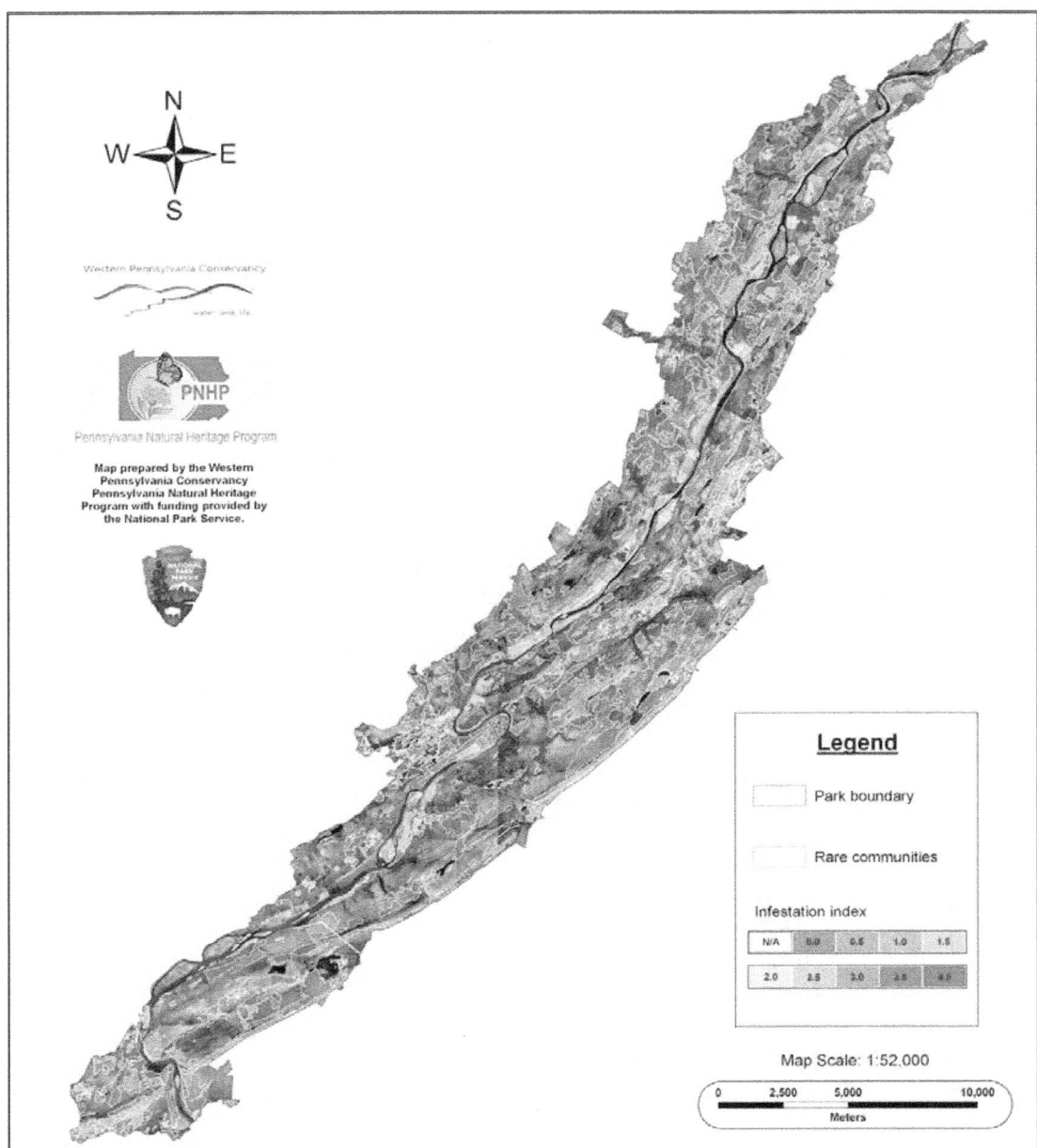

Figure 22. Infestation index of vegetation communities in the Delaware Water Gap National Recreation Area.

Discussion

Overall, the accuracy assessment and modeling data suggests invasive exotic plant species are not completely ubiquitous but certainly present within Delaware Water Gap National Recreation Area. Based on the accuracy assessment points, it appears a large portion of the park contained few invasive species (Table 5). None of the individual models predicted greater than 35% of the park as potentially suitable habitat for each given species. However, collectively, the distribution models predicted 59% of the park as potential habitat. The results suggest the park is in need of extensive invasive species management.

Invasive species tended to exhibit certain patterns within the park. Areas of high invasive activity appear to be associated with successional areas, such as regenerating forests and agricultural fields, as well as riparian and mesic terrestrial forests. These habitats provide light availability and mesic conditions that appear to be preferred by the invasive species. It is important to note that most native species would proliferate from these conditions as well; however, such species are typically outcompeted by invasive species. Areas of low invasive activity appear to be cliff complexes and dry terrestrial communities. Such communities are well drained to drought prone and may not satisfy the soil moisture preference that invasive species seem to exhibit. Rare communities that tended to have a higher mean invasive index were habitats with rich, mesic conditions, such as fens and riverside rock outcrops but also some scree slopes which offer high light availability. Given the rarity of these communities, efforts should be concentrated on invasive species management at these sites and the surrounding communities.

The maximum entropy models tend to best represent potential distributions within the park, based on model evaluation results. Japanese barberry (*Berberis thunbergii*), winged euonymus (*Euonymus alatus*), and tree-of-heaven (*Ailanthus altissima*) were the most widely predicted of the target species. This is probably due to broader habitat preferences of these species when compared to the other species modeled with maximum entropy. For example, Japanese barberry and winged euonymus can grow in a variety of soil and light conditions, while common reed (*Phragmites australis*) is typically restricted to wet communities. All species in this modeling method appear to have moderate accuracy, based on the measures of model performance, with a few exceptions. Japanese barberry and winged euonymus had higher rates of test commission and omission which resulted in lower true skill statistics (TSS). This may be a result of these two species having a broad range of habitat tolerances which the model was unable to compensate for, or an important variable was overlooked in the modeling process. In general, sample size appears to increase accuracy with these models. For example, the *A. altissima* model had a considerably lower percent test omission error, lower test commission error, and higher TSS compared to *C. biebersteinii* and *E. alatus*.

The heuristic models, in general, represent plausible distributions of invasive species within the park. For species within this modeling approach, the results suggest that the modeled distributions are accurately predicted with the exception of *Acer platanoides*. *A. platanoides* had a considerably high test omission error and low TSS value, most likely due to the small test sample size for occurrences (n=3). However, for this modeling approach, the overall accuracy score is more biased towards the absence data used to test the model due to low sample sizes or lack of presence data to test the models. Ideally, these models should be evaluated using more presence data but could be used to guide future surveys for these species.

Although the models appear to be fairly accurate in prediction, several caveats need to be taken into consideration when interpreting the results. Maximum entropy distribution maps are data dependent and are subjected to biases contained in the data (such as sampling data not addressing the full range of habitat preferences for the species). The environmental drivers for the species may be an artifact of the data and may not reflect actual ecological significance. Such a variable may fit the data very well and not be representative of a habitat preference or requirement. It is possible that vegetation community, which was consistently the most important driver for all maximum entropy models, could be an artifact variable, but it is more likely the communities are a combination of environmental and biotic variables such as seral stage, soil moisture, mycorrhizal associations, and the inability of the associated vegetation to outcompete invasive species. While the vegetation layer certainly refines the models in terms of the predicted outcome, it is still possible to predict coarser invasive species' distributions without a vegetation community data layer. The heuristic models are based on expert knowledge and therefore may not fully address the habitat variables that restrict a species' distribution. This would account for the large amount of predicted area for these species, given certain limiting variables are currently not incorporated. Additionally, these models are completely data independent in the statistical sense and may be subject to biases made on expert's assumptions.

Several management recommendations can be provided based on this study. We suggest efforts should be concentrated at species modeled using maximum entropy, given known ocurrences are more frequent within the park and considered an immediate threat. Based upon the model and accuracy assessment results, Japanese barberry (*Berberis thunbergii*) appears to be the most widespread species throughout the park and may pose considerable threats to natural resources. However, given the breadth of the *B. thunbergii*'s distribution within the park, it may be more beneficial to concentrate efforts where other species overlap with *B. thunbergii*. Additionally, while tree-of-heaven (*Ailanthus altissima*) appears to be one of the most widespread of these species and should be therefore be considered a priority, it can often be difficult to manage, given the ability to reproduce via clonal growth. More restricted species, such as *Verbascum thapsus*, *Centaurea biebersteinii*, and *Phragmites australis*, had lower predicted distributions, given their habitat preferences, so it may be more beneficial to target areas where these species are concentrated versus a species that occurs in multiple conditions across the park. Species modeled via heuristic models are currently not frequent in the park but appear to have a potentially large distribution. Therefore, it may be beneficial to establish monitoring plots and/or survey routes in areas where these species were predicted to occur. Rare communities and areas of high resource value should also be given priority. However, it is important to utilize appropriate measures of control to limit the disturbances of the native communities where invasive species occur. Overall, several of these species may be managed at one time by targeting areas of high infestation, such as successional, riparian, and mesic terrestrial forests. Areas with a large number of overlapping distributions include areas near Milford, Minisink Island, Namanock Island, Dingman's Ferry, south of Shapnack Island, Bushkill Creek, Depew Island, Poxono Island, Depue Island, Brodhead Creek, and the New Jersey portion of the park adjacent to Arrow Island.

The model for susceptibility of eastern hemlock (*Tsuga canadensis*) communities to invasion suggests that *T. canadensis* communities in DEWA are currently at a moderate risk to invasion. Overall, the *T. canadensis* communities are currently minimally invaded with a few sites degraded by invasive species. The spatial distribution of these communities shows that the majority of them are situated in fairly intact forest complexes. It appears that *T. canadensis* communities adjacent to successional, riparian, and mesic terrestrial communities had a higher index value, indicating a higher susceptibility to invasion. Such results are most likely related to higher light availability and mesic conditions. However, these results are static and do not predict future changes in canopy cover that would provide the light availability required for invasive plant species.

According to the eastern hemlock analysis, several areas of hemlock stands may be targeted for monitoring and management of invasive species following hemlock woolly adelgid infestations. Areas in most danger include stand complexes located at the mouth of Conashaugh Creek, mouth of Dingmans Creek, and Little and Big Bushkill creeks, as well as many isolated or smaller stands, especially along the Delaware River or adjacent to developed areas such as Milford, 209/206 interchange, Cliff Park Inn, Delaware Water Gap boro, and the water gap itself. Moderate to highly susceptible areas include the Raymondskill drainage, most of Dingmans Creek, Broadhead-Heller Creek, Mill Creek, and Toms Creek. In addition, the Eastern Hemlock Forests have inherently greater susceptibility to invasive plants than the mixed hemlock types if widespread hemlock decline or mortality continues. Of the 53 Eastern Hemlock Forest polygons, 19 polygons have a Susceptibility Index > 1.5 (greater than average), so these areas might be targeted for monitoring or management.

Literature Cited

Alouche, O., A. Tsoar and R. Kadmon. 2006. Assessing the accuracy of species distribution models: prevalence, kappa and the true test statistic (TSS). Journal of Applied Ecology 43:1223–1232.

Amsberry, L, M. A. Baker, P. J. Ewanchuk, and M. D. Bertness. 2000. Clonal integration and the expansion of *Phragmites australis*. Ecological Applications 10:1110–1118.

Beers, T. W., P. E. Dress, and L. C. Wensel. 1966. Aspect transformation in site productivity research. Journal of Forestry 64:691–692.

Brothers, T. S., and A. Spingarn. 1992. Forest fragmentation and alien plant invasion of central Indiana old-growth forests. Conservation Biology 6:91–100.

Carmel, Y., R. Kadmon, and R. Nirel. 2001. Spatiotemporal predictive models of Mediterranean vegetation dynamics. Ecological Applications 11:268–280.

Cassidy, T. M., J. H. Fownes, and R. A. Harrington. 2004. Nitrogen limits an invasive perennial shrub in forest understory. Biological Invasions 6:113–121.

Chamblin, H. D., P. B. Wood, and J. W. Edwards. 2004. Allegheny woodrat (*Neotoma magister*) use of rock drainage channels on reclaimed mines in southern West Virginia. American Midland Naturalist 151:346–354.

Collingham, Y. C., R. A. Wadsworth, B. Huntley, and P. E. Hulme. 2000. Predicting the spatial distribution of non-indigenous riparian weeds: issues of spatial scale and extent. Journal of Applied Ecology 37:13–27.

Cusick, A. W. 1993. Scientific note: *Cardamine impatiens* and *Sibaria virginica* (Brassicaceae) in West Virginia. Castanea 58:301–302.

Davis, E. S., P. K. Fay, T. K, Chicoine, and C.A. Lacey. 1993. Persistence of spotted knapweed (*Centaurea maculosa*) seed in soil. Weed Science 41:57–61.

Ehrenfeld, J. G. 1997. Invasion of deciduous forest preserves in the New York metropolitan region by Japanese barberry (*Berberis thunbergii* DC,). Journal of the Torrey Botanical Society 124:210–215.

Elith, J., C. H. Graham, R. P. Anderson, M. Dudik, S. Ferrier, A. Guisan, R. J. Hijmans, F. Huettmna, J. R. Leathwick, A. Lehmann, J. Li, L. G. Lohmann, B. A. Loiselle, G. Manion, C. Moritz, M. Nakamura, Y. Nakazawa, J. M. Overton, A. T. Peterson, S. J. Phillips, K. Richardson, R. Scachetti-Pereira, R. E. Schapire, J. Soberon, S. Williams, M. S. Wisz, and N. E. Zimmerman. 2006. Novel methods improve prediction of species' distributions from occurrence data. Ecography 29:129–151.

Fielding, A. H., and J. F. Bell. 1997. A review of methods for the assessment of prediction errors in conservation presence/absence models. Environmental Conservation 24:38–49.

Franklin, J. 1998. Predicting the distribution of shrub species in southern California from climate and terrain-derived variables. Journal of Vegetation Science 9:733–748.

Goldblum, D., and S. W. Beatty. 1999. Influence of an old field/forest edge on a northeastern United States deciduous forest understory community. Journal of the Torrey Botanical Society 126:335–343.

Gross, K. L., and P. A. Werner. 1982. Colonizing abilities of biennial plant species in relation to ground cover: implications for their distributions in a successional sere. Ecology 63:921–931.

Guisan, A., and N. E. Zimmerman. 2000. Predictive habitat distribution models in ecology. Ecological Modelling 135:147–186.

Harper, K. A., E. MacDonald, P. J. Burton, J. Chen, K. D. Brosofske, S. C. Saunders, E. S. Euskirchen, D. Roberts, M. S. Jaiteh, and P. Esseen. 2005. Edge influence on forest structure and composition in fragmented landscapes. Conservation Biology 19:768–782.

Harrington, R. A., J. H. Fownes, and T. M. Cassidy. 2004. Japanese barberry (Berberis thunbergii) in forest understory: leaf and whole plant responses to nitrogen availability. American Midland Naturalist 151:206–216.

Hauber, D. P., D. A. White, S. P. Powers, and F. R. DeFrancesh. 1991. Isozyme variation and correspondence with unusual infrared reflectance patterns in Phragmites australis (Poaceae). Plant Systematics and Evolution 178:1–8.

Hernandez, P. A., C. H. Graham, L. L. Master, and D. L. Albert. 2006. The effect of sample size and species characteristics on performance of different species distribution modeling methods. Ecography 29:773–785.

Hiebert, R. D. 1997. Prioritizing invasive plants and planning for management. In J. O. Luken and J. W. Thieret, eds. Assessment and Management of Plant Invasions. Springer-Verlag. New York, NY.

Hiebert, R. D., and J. Stubbendieck. 1993. Handbook for ranking exotic plants for management and control. NPS, Midwest Regional Office, Omaha, NE. Natural Resources Report NPS/NRMWRO/NRR–93/08.

Huebner, C. D, C. McQuattie, and J. Rebbeck. 2007. Mycorrhizal associations in Ailanthus altissima (Simaroubaceae) from forested and non-forested sites. Journal of the Torrey Botanical Society 134:27–33.

Iverson, L. R., and A. M. Prasad. 1998. Predicting abundance of 80 tree species following climate change in the eastern United States. Ecological Monographs 68:465–485.

Kivilaan, M., and R. S. Bandurski. 1973. The ninety-year period for Dr. Beal's seed viability experiment. American Journal of Botany 60:140–145.

Kloeppel, B. D., and M. D. Abrams. 1995. Ecophysiological attributes of the native *Acer saccharum* and the exotic *Acer platanoides* in urban oak forests in Pennsylvania, USA. Tree Physiology 15:739–746.

Knapp, L. B., and C. D. Canham. 2000. Invasion of an old-growth forest in New York by *Ailanthus altissima*: sapling growth and recruitment in canopy gaps. Journal of the Torrey Botanical Society 127:307–315.

Kourtev, P. S., W. Z. Huang, and J. G. Ehrenfeld. 1999. Differences in earthworm densities and nitrogen dynamics in soils under exotic and native plant species. Biological Invasions 1:237–245.

Kowarik, I. 1995. Clonal growth in *Ailanthus altissima* on a natural site in West Virginia. Journal of Vegetation Science 6:853–856.

Kumar, V., and A. DiTommaso. 2005. Mile-a-minute (*Polygonum perfoliatum*): an increasingly problematic invasive species. Weed Technology 19:1071–1077.

Lawerence, J. G., A. Colwell, and O. J. Sexton. 1991. The ecological impact of allelopathy in *Ailanthus altissima* (Simaroubaceae). American Journal of Botany 78:948–958.

Lees, B. G., and K. Ritman. 1991. Decision-tree and rule-induction approach to integration of remotely sensed and GIS data in mapping vegetation in disturbed or hilly environments. Environmental Management 15:823–831.

Locken, L. J., and R. G. Kelsey. 1987. Cnicin concentrations in *Centaurea maculosa*, spotted knapweed. Biochemical Systematics and Ecology 15:313–320.

Manel, S., H. C. Williams, and S. J. Ormerod. 2001. Evaluating presence-absence models in ecology: the need to account for prevalence. Journal of Applied Ecology 38:921–931.

Marshall, M. R., and N. B. Piekielek. 2007. Eastern Rivers and Mountains Network Ecological Monitoring Plan. Natural Resource Report NPS/ERMN/NRR—2007/017. National Park Service. Fort Collins, CO.

Matlack, G. R. 1993. Microenvironment variation within and among deciduous forest edge sites in the eastern United States. Biological Conservation 66:185–194.

Matlack, G. R. 1994. Vegetation dynamics of the forest edge-trends in space and successional time. Journal of Ecology 82:113–123.

McNab, W. H. 1989. Terrain shape index: quantifying effect of minor landforms on tree height. Forest Science 35:91–104.

Mehrhoff, L. J., J. A. Silander Jr., S. A. Leicht, E. S. Mosher, and N. M. Tabak. 2003. IPANE: Invasive Plant Atlas of New England. Department of Ecology & Evolutionary Biology. University of Connecticut. Storrs, CT. http://www.ipane.org.

Meiners, S. J., and S. T. A. Pickett. 1999. Changes in community and population responses across a forest-field gradient. Ecography 22:261–267.

Mladenoff, D. J., T. A. Sickley, R. G. Haight, and A. P. Wydeven. 1995. A regional landscape analysis and prediction of favorable wolf habitat in the northern great lakes region. Conservation Biology 9:279–294.

Moore D. M., B. G. Lees, and S. M. Davey. 1991. A new method for predicting vegetation distributions using decision tree analysis in a geographic information system. Environmental Management 15:59–71.

Morse, L. E., J. M. Randall, N. Benton, R. Hiebert, and S. Lu. 2004. An invasive species assessment protocol: evaluating non-native plants for their impact on biodiversity. Version 1. NatureServe. Arlington, VA.

Mountain, W. L. 1989. Mile-a-minute (*Polygonum perfoliatum* L.) update-distribution, biology and control suggestions. Pennsylvania Department of Agriculture Weed Circular 15.

Oliver, J. D. 1996. Mile-a-minute weed (*Polygonum perfoliatum* L.), an invasive vine in natural and disturbed sites. Castanea 61:244–251.

Orrock, J. L., J. F. Pagels, W. J. McShea, and E. K. Harper. 1999. Predicting presence and abundance of a small mammal species: the effect of scale and resolutions. Ecological Applications 10:1356–1366.

Orwig, D. A., and D. R. Foster. 1998. Forest response to the introduced hemlock woolly adelgid in southern New England, USA. Journal of the Torrey Botanical Society 125:60–73.

Parendes, L. A., and J. A. Jones. 2000. Role of light availability and dispersal in exotic plant invasion along roads and streams in the H. J. Andrews Experimental Forest, Oregon. Conservation Biology 14:64–75.

Pearson, R. G., C. J. Raxworthy, M. Nakamura, and A. T. Peterson. 2007. Predicting species' distributions from small numbers of occurrence records: a test case using cryptic geckos in Madagascar. Journal of Biogeography 34:102–117.

Pereira, J. M. C., and R. M. Itami. 1991. GIS-based habitat modeling using logistic multiple regression: a study of the Mt. Graham red squirrel. Photogrammetric Engineering and Remote Sensing 57:1475–1486.

Perles, S. J., G. S. Podniesinski, E. Eastman, L.A. Sneddon, and S. C. Gawler. 2007. Classification and mapping of vegetation and fire fuel models at Delaware Water Gap National Recreation Area. Technical Report NPS/NER/NRTR—2007/076. National Park Service. Philadelphia, PA.

Perles, S. J., G. S. Podniesinski, M. Furedi, B. A. Eichelberger, A. Feldman, G. Edinger, E. Eastman and L. A. Sneddon. 2008. Vegetation Classification and Mapping at Upper Delaware Scenic and Recreational River. Technical Report NPS/NER/NRTR— 2008/133. National Park Service. Philadelphia, PA.

Phillips, S. J., R. P. Anderson, and R. E. Schapire. 2006. Maximum entropy modeling of species geographic distributions. Ecological Modelling 190:231–259.

Reinartz, J. A. 1984. Life history variation of common mullein (*Verbascum thapsus*): I. latitudinal differences in population dynamics and timing of reproduction. Journal of Ecology 72:897–912.

Rhoads, A. F., and T. A. Block. 2007. The plants of Pennsylvania: an illustrated manual: 2nd edition. University of Pennsylvania Press. Philadelphia, PA.

Riefner, R. E., and D. R. Windler. 1979. *Polygonum perfoliatum* established in Maryland. Castanea 44:91–93.

Searcy, K. B., C. Pucko, and D. McClelland. 2006. The distribution and habitat preferences of introduced species in the Mount Holyoke range, Hampshire Co., Massachusetts. Rhodora 108:43–61.

Semenza, R. J., J. A. Young, and R. A. Evans. 1978. Influence of light and temperature on the germination and seed bed ecology of common mullein (*Verbascum thapsus*). Weed Science 26:577–581.

Silander, J. A., and D. M. Klepeis. 1999. The invasion ecology of Japanese barberry (*Berberis thunbergii*) in the New England landscape. Biological Invasions 1:189–201.

Spears, B. M., S. T. Rose, and W. S. Belles. 1980. Effect of canopy cover, seeding depth, and soil moisture on emergence of *Centaurea maculosa* and *C. diffusa*. Weed Research 20:87–90.

Taverna, K., D. L. Urban, and R. I. McDonald. 2004. Modeling landscape vegetation pattern in response to historic land-use: a hypothesis-driven approach for the North Carolina Piedmont, USA. Landscape Ecology 20:689–702.

United States Department of Agriculture (USDA). 2002. Invasive species identification sheet-narrowleaf bittercress. http://www.ct.nrcs.usda.gov/invas-factsheets.html.

Vitousek, P. M., C. M. D'Antionio, L. L. Loope, and R. Westbrooks. 1996. Biological invasions as global environmental change. American Scientist 84:468–478.

Watson, A. K., and A. J. Renney. 1974. The biology of Canadian weeds. *Centaurea diffusa* and *C. maculosa*. Canadian Journal of Plant Science 54:687–701.

Webb, S. L., T. H. Pendergat, and M. Dwyer. 2001. Response of native and exotic maple seedlings banks to removal of exotic, invasive Norway maple (*Acer platanoides*). Journal of the Torrey Botanical Society 128:141–149.

Wu, X. B., and F. E. Smeins. 2000. Multiple-scale habitat modeling approach for rare plant conservation. Landscape and Urban Planning 51:11–28.

Wyckoff, P. H., and S. L. Webb. 1996. Understory influence of the invasive Norway maple (*Acer platanoides*). Bulletin of the Torrey Botanical Club 123:197–205.

Young, R. F., K. S. Shields, and G. P. Berlyn. 1995. Hemlock woolly adelgid (*Homoptera, Adelgidae*): stylet bundle insertion and feeding sites. Annals of Entomological Society of America 88:827–835.

Zimmerman, N. E., and F. Kienast. 1999. Predictive mapping of alpine grasslands in Switzerland: species versus community approach. Journal of Vegetation Science 10:469–482.

Appendix A. Photographs of study species.

Figure A1. Tree-of-heaven (*Ailanthus altissima*). Photograph taken by Shana Stewart, Pennsylvania Natural Heritage Program.

Figure A2. Winged euonymus (*Euonymus alatus*). Photograph taken by Rocky Gleason, Pennsylvania Natural Heritage Program.

Figure A3. Common reed (*Phragmites australis*). Photograph taken by Andrew Strassman, Pennsylvania Natural Heritage Program.

Figure A4. Mile-a-minute (*Polygonum perfoliatum*). Photograph taken by Rocky Gleason, Pennsylvania Natural Heritage Program.

Figure A5. Mile-a-minute (*Polygonum perfoliatum*) infestation. Photograph taken by Andrew Strassman, Pennsylvania Natural Heritage Program.

Figure A6. Japanese hops (*Humulus japonicus*). Photograph taken by Rocky Gleason, Pennsylvania Natural Heritage Program.

Figure A7. Hemlock woolly adelgid (*Adelgis tsugae*). Photograph taken by Division of Forest Pest Management, Pennsylvania Department of Conservation and Natural Resources.

Figure A8. Eastern hemlock (*Tsuga canadensis*) tree mortality following hemlock woolly adelgid (*Adelgis tsugae*) infestation. Photograph taken by Division of Forest Pest Management, Pennsylvania Department of Conservation and Natural Resources.

Appendix B. List of GIS deliverables.

Folder	Subfolder	Name	Description
Base_data	-	dewa_all_orthos_match.sid	Aerial imagery of DEWA.
		DEWA_boundry.shp	Boundary of DEWA.
		White_out.shp	Mask for boundary.
Communities	Hemlock	Hemlock.shp	Hemlock communities in DEWA with susceptibility index.
	Vegetation_comm	Rare_communities.shp	Rare vegetation communities.
		Vegetation_comm.shp	Vegetation communities with infestation index.
Species	Acer_plat	Acer_platanoides.shp	Presence points for *Acer platanoides*.
		Acer_platanoides_.shp	Predicted distribution for *Acer platanoides*.
	Aila_alti	Ailanthus_altissima.shp	Presence points for *Ailanthus altissima*.
		Ailanthus_altissima_.shp	Predicted distribution for *Ailanthus altissima*.
	All_Species	All_species.shp	Overlapping areas for sprecies' predicted distributions.
		All_species_points.shp	Accuracy assessment points with abundance values for invasive species within DEWA.
	Berb_thun	Berberis_thunbergii.shp	Presence points for *Berberis thunbergii*.
		Berberis_thunbergii_.shp	Predicted distribution for *Berberis thunbergii*
	Card_impa	Cardamine_impatiens_.shp	Predicted distribution for *Cardamine impatiens*.
	Cent_bieb	Centaurea_biebersteinii.shp	Presence points for *Centaurea biebersteinii*.
		Centaurea_biebersteinii_.shp	Predicted distribution for *Centaurea biebersteinii*.
	Euon_alat	Euonymus_alatus.shp	Presence points for *Euonymus alatus*.
		Euonymus_alatus_.shp	Predicted distribution for *Euonymus alatus*.
	Humu_japo	Humulus_japonicus.shp	Presence points for *Humulus japonicus*.
		Humulus_japonicus_.shp	Predicted distribution for *Humulus japonicus*.
	Phra_aust	Phragmites_australis.shp	Presence points for *Phragmites australis*.
		Phragmites_australis_.shp	Predicted distribution for *Phragmites australis*.
	Poly_perf	Polygonum_perfoliatum.shp	Presence points for *Polygonum perfoliatum*.
		Polygonum_perfoliatum_.shp	Predicted distribution for *Polygonum perfoliatum*.
	Ranu_fica	Ranunculus_ficaria_.shp	Predicted distribution for *Ranunculus ficaria*.
	Verb_thap	Verbascum_thapsus.shp	Presence points for *Verbascum thapsus*.
		Verbascum_thapsus_.shp	Predicted distribution for *Verbascum thapsus*.

NPS D-303 February 2009